HOPES FOR GREAT HAPPENINGS

by the same author

in the Modern Theatre Profiles series
ARDEN: A Study of His Plays

in the Methuen Young Drama series
John Ford's Cuban Missile Crisis (ed.)

*The Russian Revolution staged in the streets of Bradford — the
Cuban Missile Crisis seen as a John Ford movie — an investigation
of Bradford pentecostals that developed into an indictment of
civilian bombing raids — a wide range of research projects, games,
exhibitions, theatrical cartoons. . .*

*Between 1965 and 1973 a unique experiment in radical education
took place at the Regional College of Art, Bradford. When Albert
Hunt joined the staff in 1965, he found himself virtually creating
his own syllabus — working mostly with 'non-academic' students
on a fascinating range of games, projects and theatre events right
outside the main stream of exam-oriented education.*

*In this highly personal book, Albert Hunt describes how he himself
evolved from a conventional grammar school teacher into the
animator of such work; he gives a blow-by-blow account of many
of the events themselves; and, in particular, he describes the
evolution of new working relationships between teachers and
students, which in turn point forward to an alternative way of
looking at society.*

Hopes for Great Happenings *is not only a vividly interesting account
of Albert Hunt's teaching methods but is of practical value to anybody involved in liberal studies, in theatre or in community arts
work. And at a time of educational and cultural crisis, it offers a
positive contribution to the development of a theory and practice
of permanent education.*

HOPES FOR GREAT HAPPENINGS

Alternatives in education and theatre

Albert Hunt

Eyre Methuen London

First published in 1976
Copyright © Albert Hunt 1976
Printed in Great Britain
for Eyre Methuen Ltd
11 New Fetter Lane London EC4P 4EE
by Fletcher & Son Ltd, Norwich

ISBN   0 413 30670 4 (Hardback)
         0 413 30680 1 (Paperback)

The photograph on the front cover shows Chris Vine in The Workhouse Donkey *and is reproduced by courtesy of Paul Clamp. The photograph on the back cover is reproduced by courtesy of N.O.S. Television.*

Errata

page x	'Paul Binnaerts' (line 13) should be Paul Binnerts.
page 3	The book referred to in line 24 is *Drama and Society in the Age of Jonson* by L. C. Knights.
page 21	Lines 3-4 should read '. . . received phrases gummed together.'
page 49	'Donal Gee' (line 34) should be Donald Gee.
page 73	'John Lathan' (line 29) should be John Latham.
page 156	Line 26 should refer to 'well-publicised radicals'.
page 173	Line 8 of Grandmother's Footsteps should read: 'The sense was of grotesques noisily playing . . .'
page 176	'departmental students' (line 12) should read 'departmental tutors'.
page 193	The poem is by Angela Shepherd.

To my father.

Dirty frogs want to feed on crane,
Poor scum hope for great happenings in vain.
Look at yourself in some ditch water, do!
What great deeds can be done by the likes of you?
Can snow fall in mid-July?
Can the sun rise in the western sky?

Landlord Ts'ui from the opera
Wang Kuei and Li Hsiang-hsiang

On a beam which supports the ceiling of Brecht's study are
painted the words, 'Truth is Concrete'. On a window-sill
stands a small wooden donkey which can nod its head.
Brecht has hung a little sign round its neck on which he has
written: 'Even I must understand it.'

Walter Benjamin, *Conversations With Brecht*

Contents

Illustrations

It would be impossible to thank everybody who contributed to the work described in this book. But I should like to express particular thanks to Bill Gainham, without whose encouragement and ideas I should have left Bradford before it all started; to John Gascoigne and Michael Randle, of the Complementary Studies team; to the former Principal of the Regional College of Art, Bradford, Mr F.T. Coleclough; to all the members of the Theatre Group, but particularly to Doug Lawrence and Stephanie Simpson, without whom the group, and the theatre course, would never have been launched; to Jacquie Crone, Keith Knowles, Roger Simcox and Chris Vine, who helped the group to survive far longer than most similar groups; to John Booth, to the three from Shrewsbury, Maurice Burgess, Ian Taylor and George Dorosz; to Paul Binnaerts, from Amsterdam; to Brian Winston, for his help with film and television; to Joe Dolan, who willingly took the responsibility for the full-time course; and to many other artists, including Adrian Mitchell, Adrian Henri, Tony Earnshaw, Robin Page, Patrick Hughes, Bruce Lacey, John Fox. I should also like to thank John Arden and Margaretta D'Arcy for their help and encouragement; and all the students who made the work possible by their involvement.

Acknowledgements

Acknowledgements and thanks are due for the photographs to:
The Arts Council of Great Britain and the Serpentine Gallery,
London, for 18; to Paul Clamp for 5, 7, 17; to Peter Holdsworth,
The Telegraph and Argus, Bradford for 1; to Mal Seddon for 4,
15; to Tony Senior for 3, 8, 9, 10, 11, 19; to Div Sheard for
16; to the Wroclaw Festival for 12, 13.

Acknowledgements and thanks are also due to Veronica Hussey,
Keith Knowles and Angela Shepherd for the use of their poems;
and to Adrian Mitchell and Cape Goliard Press for the lines from
'Leaflets' published in *Out Loud*; to George Sassoon for the lines
from 'The Hero' by Siegfried Sassoon; to Monthly Press Review
for the lines from the opera, 'Wang Kuei and Li Hsiang-hsiang',
published in *Fanshen*, copyright © 1966 by Willam Hinton; to
Eyre Methuen for the extract from Brecht's *The Caucasian Chalk
Circle* translated by James and Tania Stern (copyright in the
original work © 1954 by Suhrkamp Verlag, Berlin); to John
Willett for the extracts from *Brecht on Theatre* published by
Eyre Methuen.

The line from 'Washing on the Siegfried Line', written by Michael
Carr and Jimmy Kennedy is reproduced by kind permission of
Peter Maurice Music Co. Ltd; the line from 'We'll Meet Again', by
Ross Parker and Hugh Charles, is reproduced by permission of
Dash Music Co. Ltd; the line from 'I'd like to teach the world to
sing' is reproduced by permission of Dick James Music Ltd; the
line from 'Run, rabbit, run' is used by permission of Noel Gay
Music; the verse beginning 'Lord, send the old time power' is
used by kind permission of the copyright owner, Roacheaver Co.,
USA. No copyright owners have been traced for the lines,
'There is a rose that grows in no man's land' and 'Take myself,
and I will be, Ever always all for thee'. Apologies and thanks are
due to the owners if these lines are copyright material.

Part of the third section of Chapter four is based on a paper
originally submitted to the Arts Council Committee for Young
People's Theatre.

Chapter one
Portrait of the educator
as a sceptical barbarian

'The young person in school is monstrously confronted by the BARBARIAN in unforgettable form. The latter posses-ses almost limitless power. Equipped with pedagogical skills and many years of experience he trains the pupil to become a prototype of himself. The pupil learns everything required for getting ahead in the world — the very same things that are necessary to getting ahead in school: deceit, pretending to have knowledge one does not have, the ability to get even without being punished for it, speedy acquisition of clichés, subservience, a readiness to betray one's fellows to the higher-ups . . .'

Bertolt Brecht

'Men are products of circumstances and upbringing, and therefore changed men are products of other circumstances and changed upbringing, but circumstances are changed precisely by men and the educator himself must be educated.'

Karl Marx

1

Why complementary studies? Because, ironically, 'they' said so — 'they' being, in this case, the National Advisory Council on Art Education whose first report (the Cold-stream Report) was published in 1960.

The Council had been set up to 'advise . . . on all aspects of art education in establishments of further education', and to devise a course which 'would approximate in quality and standard of achievement to a university course of the same length leading to a degree'. Their report recommended the establishment of a new award, the Diploma in Art and Design, (Dip.A.D.), which would have the status of a university degree; and the setting up of a number of nationally recognised centres, which would offer courses leading to this award. Individual colleges were invited to devise their own syllabuses and submit them for recognition.

The Coldstream Council laid it down that, 'all diploma courses should include complementary studies. By this,' the report went on, 'we mean any non-studio subjects, in addition to the history of art, which may strengthen or give breadth to the students' training. We do not think that any specific subjects should be prescibed. The only criterion. . . is that these studies should be genuinely complementary and helpful to the main object — the study of art.' The report expressed the hope that 'the complementary studies will give scope for practising written and spoken English', and recommended that 'about 15 per cent of the total course should be devoted to the history of art and complementary studies.'

The publication of the report was followed by the establishment, in 1961, of the Summerson Council, to decide which colleges should be recognised as Dip.A.D. centres — and by a mad scramble for recognition by the colleges themselves. As part of the scramble, many colleges created departments of complementary studies and appointed highly qualified university graduates to run them.

And this was how, in May 1965, I came to join the staff of the Regional College of Art, Bradford. I was appointed to direct the complementary studies section of a new Dip.A.D. course. It was confidently expected that the course would begin the following September.

2

The syllabus for the new course had been invented long before I arrived. The subject that was being offered was a study of the relationship of the artist to society throughout history. At first sight, it looked impressive.

Using as key texts Richard Hoggart's *The Uses of Literacy* and Arnold Hauser's *Social History of Art*, the students would examine the way social and economic factors had shaped the development of art at different periods in different kinds of society. They would concentrate on three periods, beginning with the twentieth century, then jumping back to the Renaissance, and coming forward again to the Industrial Revolution. There would be lectures and seminars each week, and the art history lectures would be integrated with the general course. There was a formidable reading list.

On paper, the course was a typical, well-worked out example of academic planning. But studying it, before I took up my appointment, I had a number of misgivings.

They were partly connected with the amount of time available. The syllabus could easily, it seemed to me, have formed the basis of a full-time university course. We were asking these art students to cover it in 15 per cent of their time. Moreover, it could be assumed that many of these students had chosen to go to art college rather than university, because they didn't regard themselves as scholars. Even to a university post-graduate the reading list would have been daunting.

But, more fundamentally, I questioned the educational validity of the subject itself. I had just been reading L.C. Knight's *Drama in the Age of Jonson*. Knight tries to relate the forms of Elizabethan theatre to mediaeval economics. I'd found the book illuminating — but I'd also felt that if I'd really known very much about mediaeval economics, I should have wanted to question much of what it said.

The book had been written by a specialist who had devoted a lot of time and energy to studying one tiny corner of the complex relationship between art and society, and had eventually reached some speculative conclusions. Yet we were going to ask art students to cover, in 15 per cent of their time, the same subject stretched out over several centuries.

The effect of such a course, it seemed to me, could only be to dole out scraps of knowledge, which would be so superficial as to be useless. What, for example, could anybody really learn from 'Week 11: Science in the Twentieth Century', and 'Week 12: Religion in the Twentieth Century'?

My first job at Bradford, I thought, would be to try to make something workable out of this academic abstraction. But before I was faced with this problem, the syllabus had become irrelevant.

A month after I arrived, we heard that Bradford was not going to be given the Dip.A.D. The course I'd been recruited to run never even started.

3

At first, I saw this as something of a disaster. I'd been brought to Bradford to do advanced work: now I was to be faced with 'vocational' students, none of whom could be expected to be interested in 'academic' work. Many of them had no GCEs at all. They had been grammar-school 'failures', or they had come from secondary modern schools, where they had been unhappy. I couldn't really expect them to have much involvement with my own concerns.

On the other hand, the failure to be given Dip.A.D. did, at least, remove one problem. I no longer had to struggle to bend somebody else's syllabus to my own interests. I was free to devise another syllabus, built around what I felt myself most qualified to do.

What I felt myself most qualified to do was to teach film. This was what I'd been learning to do for several years as an adult tutor in Shropshire. I'd invented a lot of courses with a lot of different groups. I'd looked at John Ford westerns with teachers, British realist films with trades unionists, Buñuel with groups in village halls. We would look at the films together and discuss them the following week. Some of the groups had developed collective criticism of a very high standard.

It seemed to me that a study of film would form an ideal centre for the work of a complementary studies department in an art college. Film was visual: it would provide a focus to an analysis of visual language. But it was also narrative and dramatic. I saw film as an area half-way between the visual interests of art students and my own involvement with literature. We would meet in this area and learn from each other.

There were 250 full-time students. A third of these were in foundation year, and about half of *them* would leave at the end of one year to go to a Dip.A.D. centre. The rest would join the college diploma course, which was not nationally recognised. The course lasted for three years and was intended to prepare students for work in industry. There were three main areas of work: printed textiles, dress textiles and graphic design. In an attempt to keep up the numbers, entrance qualifications tended to be waived.

Most of the students came to complementary studies for one half-day a week. From my point of view, the length of time seemed to be ideal. In three hours, I would be able to show a feature film and still leave plenty of time for discussion. I planned what I imagined would be a popular course about Hollywood directors.

On the whole, the students seemed to enjoy the films. But when I tried to involve them in discussion, I met with an almost total blank. As an experienced tutor in adult education, I'd imagined that one of the expert, professional skills I'd acquired was the ability to lead a discussion. I thought I was good at that. And now I found myself doing nearly all the talking myself, with the students paying only the most passive attention.

At first I was puzzled by this. In the adult education classes in Shropshire, people had always been willing to talk about film, and they'd kept coming, week after week. They'd have stayed away if they'd been bored.

It was some time before I realised that the situations were completely different. The people in the adult education classes came because they *wanted* to. They shared a common interest. They *liked* talking about films.

The students in the art college, on the other hand, shared no such common interest. They came because they had to. It was down on their timetable. And the timetable was arranged that way for administrative, not educational, reasons. They came in those particular groups because they happened to be doing textiles or graphics together for the rest of the time, and so it was convenient to group them together for 'liberal studies'. And I had become the 'they' who was forcing them, for one half-day a week, to leave their other concerns and come and work with me.

Not that they bore me any resentment. They simply weren't interested in talking about films. They would talk about other things, though — about pubs and fights and families and abortions and the pill and the police. One of them, who wore long black hair flowing over his shoulders, told how he'd been walking about Nottingham at two o'clock in the morning when the police had picked him up and thrown him into a cell. 'You'd have thought I was one of them beatniks,' he said.

Every week I learnt a lot. But it worried me that I wasn't teaching them about film. All my education and training had taught me that I was an 'expert', a 'professional'. And I wasn't making use of my expertise.

I was, of course, to some extent right. The chit-chat about pubs and police was very friendly and informative, but it was way below the capacities of all of us. I was determined to find a way of involving the students with what I thought I had to offer.

One morning, I'd been looking at a comedy with a group of second-year textile students, and I'd tried to open up a discussion about different kinds of humour. The usual two or three students talked aimlessly for a while — some of them got involved in a meaningless wrangle. Suddenly, a girl said: 'Why do you have to spoil everything for us? The film was all right. Why do we have to sit here taking it to pieces?'

We broke for coffee. After the break there would still be an hour and a half to go. I too felt that I couldn't stand another session of aimless talk. I went into the library and found a few copies of Brecht's *The Caucasian Chalk Circle*.

When the students came back, I turned with them to one page of script — I'd already discovered with groups that it could be very laborious to try and read plays: much of the reading was so hesitant and boring that the plays fell flat. So I chose a very short scene — the one in which Grusha, the peasant girl who is running away with the Governor's baby, arrives at an old man's hut. She knocks at the door and asks for milk.

THE OLD MAN: Milk? We haven't any milk. The soldiers from the city took our goats. If you want milk, go to the soldiers.

GRUSHA: But Grandpa, you surely have a mug of milk for a child?

THE OLD MAN: And for a 'God Bless You', eh?

GRUSHA: Who said anything about a 'God Bless You'? *She pulls out her purse.* We're going to pay like princes . . . *The peasant goes off grumbling to fetch milk.* And how much is this mug?

THE OLD MAN: Three piastres. Milk has gone up.

GRUSHA: Three piastres for that drop? *Without a word the old man slams the door in her face.* Michael, did you hear that? Three piastres! We can't afford that. *She goes back, sits down again and gives the child her breast.* Well, we must try again like this. Suck. Think of the three piastres. There's nothing there, but you think you're drinking, and that's something. *Shaking her head, she realises the child has stopped sucking. She gets up, walks back to the door, and knocks again.* Open, Grandpa, we'll pay. *Under her breath:* May God strike you! *When the old man appears again:* I thought it would be half a piastre. But the child must have something. What about one piastre?

THE OLD MAN: Two.

GRUSHA: Don't slam the door again. *She rummages a long time in her purse.* Here are two piastres. But this milk has got to last. We still have a long journey ahead of us. These are cut-throat prices. It's a sin.

THE OLD MAN: If you want milk, kill the soldiers.

GRUSHA *letting the child drink:* That's an expensive joke. Drink, Michael. This is half a week's pay. The people here think we've earned our money sitting on our bottom. Michael, Michael, I certainly took on a nice burden with you! *Looking at the brocade coat in which the child is wrapped:* A brocade coat worth 1000 piastres, and not one piastre for milk.

We read the passage, and then I asked the girl who'd objected to the film discussion to 'produce' the scene. I advised
them not to try and act the scene by reading from the book,
but to improvise on what they could remember. Somebody
could be in charge of the book and after each improvisation
should say what had been left out. Then I went to the back
of the room and watched.

They organised themselves very quickly. They built a
cottage with a table and chairs. A girl's handbag became the
baby and a cup that had been filled with paint was used for
the milk.

During the next hour, everybody tried the scene in turn.
At first, they concentrated on working their way from a
rough improvisation through to the correct script. The boy
in charge of the book would point out that a certain line
had been left out. 'But it wasn't important', somebody
would say — and another would argue, 'Yes it was because
it showed. . .' They discussed every line that was there.
After about half an hour they were almost word perfect.
They'd agreed that not many lines could be spared from
the scene.

At this point, they began, almost unconsciously, to inter-
pret the scene. They did what most conventional producers
would have done: they turned it into a scene about a miserly old peasant and a motherly girl.

After one of the improvisations, I intervened. I called
aside two of the toughest boys and asked them to be
soldiers. The next time the scene began, they were to go to
the Old Man's hut, knock on the door, and, when the Old
Man appeared, break in and smash everything up. I asked
the girl playing Grusha to go to the door as soon as the
soldiers went away.

The boy who was playing the Old Man had been busy
arranging his house. He had no idea what had been planned.
He sat with his back to the rest of the group and waited for
Grusha to arrive.

There was a knock at the door. The boy turned around.
He was working hard at creating the character of an old
miserly peasant. The boys playing the soldiers kicked the
door out of the way, knocked over the chair, and systema-

tically smashed everything up. Then they overturned the table and left.

Grusha went and knocked. The boy playing the Old Man looked up. He still wasn't sure what was happening, and half-expected to be knocked about again. 'Grandpa', said the girl, 'could I have a little mug of milk?' The boy straightened up. 'The soldiers took the milk', he said. 'If you want milk, go to the soldiers.' He'd forgotten all about trying to be a miserly peasant. He was showing genuine indignation about the way he'd been treated. When he said the soldiers had taken the milk, he wasn't making a cunning excuse, but stating a fact, which had made him both frightened and angry.

After the improvisations, we talked about Brecht. I told them about the essay in which Brecht describes how he rehearsed the scene with the Berliner Ensemble. Brecht emphasises that the scene isn't about a miserly peasant and a motherly girl, but about two people behaving in a particular way in a particular situation. The relationship between the characters doesn't arise from any innate characteristics, but from the position they find themselves in. The scene isn't about characters, but about the process of bargaining.

As we discussed, everybody was involved and interested. The physical introduction of the scene with the soldiers had made Brecht's point immediate and concrete. And the first piece of real analysis we'd done had started from an overturned table and chair.

At the end of the session, I asked the girl producer why she had to spoil everything by taking it to pieces. But, of course, the analogy wasn't fair. There was clearly a difference between working at a text which had never been anything more than the skeleton for a performance, and doing a piece of critical analysis on celluloid images that were in themselves complete and unchangeable.

4

Thinking back on the Brecht session, what most struck me was the way in which we'd begun to explore intellectual ideas through physical activity. The students had been drawing on their powers of invention. But, at the same time, and as part of the same process, they had become deeply engaged in hard analysis. And the ideas had become, in Brecht's terms, 'concrete'.

About the same time a similar situation developed with a different group, almost by chance. This time the impulse came, not from a film discussion, but from the reading of a poem.

Sometimes, when there were no films available, I offered poems for discussion. I didn't try it very often, because the discussions always fell flat, and I decided that most of the students weren't interested in poetry. (Six months later, they were packing the lecture room at lunchtime to hear Adrian Mitchell, and not long after that they were booking rooms in pubs and giving readings of their own poems.)

On this occasion, I tried to discuss with a young, pre-diploma group two war poems: one by Owen, the other by Sassoon. I'd intended to do a critical comparison between the two, but I was as bored as the students were, until I had the sudden idea of asking the students to turn the poem into newspaper headlines.

The poem was called *The Hero*.

'Jack fell as he'd have wished', the Mother said,
 And folded up the letter that she'd read.
'The Colonel writes so nicely.' Something broke
 In the tired voice that wavered to a choke.
 She half looked up. 'We mothers are so proud
 Of our dead soldiers.' Then her face was bowed.

Quietly the Brother Officer went out.
He'd told the poor old dear some gallant lies
That she would cherish all her days, no doubt.
For while he coughed and mumbled, her weak eyes
Had shone with gentle triumph, brimmed with joy,
Because he'd been so brave, her glorious boy.

He thought how 'Jack', cold-footed, useless swine

Had panicked down the trench that night the mine
Went up at' Wicked Corner; how he'd tried
To get sent home, and how, at last, he'd died,
Blown to small bits. And no-one seemed to care,
Except that lonely woman with white hair.

The game was that you were to reduce the poem to a five-word headline, with a seven-word sub-title. The students worked at it for a long time: I'd never seen a group scrutinise a text so closely. The job was clearly impossible: if you could express a poem in five words there'd be no need to write the poem. But what they selected told a lot about how they read the poem. OFFICER LIES TO HERO'S MOTHER suggests a different emphasis from MOTHER'S PRIDE AT HERO'S DEATH.

We talked about the different headlines, and this led into a discussion about the characters. Did the woman really feel nothing? Why was she so careful to hide her feelings? I related her actions — lowering her eyes and folding the letter — to a whole tradition of restraint in British theatre and cinema, and further related this tradition to class attitudes, and the middle-class stranglehold on established British culture. We were, I suppose, learning about Art and Society.

At this point, the students themselves suggested acting out the poem. They immediately ran into difficulties. Both the mother and the officer were thinking things that couldn't be shown through the actions described in the poem. They solved the problem as far as the officer was concerned by inventing another officer who also had letters to deliver, and writing the officer's view of Jack into the dialogue between the two. ('Remember how he panicked down the trench that night the mine went up at Wicked Corner?')

But the mother defeated them. The problem was that the poem was partly *about* the fact that she didn't show her feelings — whereas theatre is all about showing. A lot of the girls tried out the part. They stared, motionless, like a character in close-up on film or television, trying to com-

municate that deep emotions were being felt behind the
staring eyes. They contorted their faces, twitched the
corners of their mouths. One morning, the whole group
played at trying to communicate particular emotions
through mime. They failed. We analysed pieces of film to
see whether or not experienced actors were more precise. I
told them about the Russian experimental film in which
the face of an actor, which never changed its expression,
was intercut with different objects. The meaning of the
actor's face was changed by the objects. Juxtaposed with a
plate of soup, the face expressed hunger. The analysis didn't
really help us to solve the problem of performing the poem.

When we seemed to have reached a blank wall, I fell
back again on *The Caucasian Chalk Circle.* This time we
looked at the scene in which a girl confronts her returned
soldier lover across a stream. 'So many words are said,'
writes Brecht, 'so many thoughts are left unsaid. Whence
he comes he doesn't say. Hear what he thought but didn't
say.' What the soldier thought is expressed in a song, which
is taken out of the action. The naturalistic surface is
broken: the soldier speaks 'out of character'.

The group seized eagerly on the idea. They invented a
narrator. They wrote the Colonel's letter: 'Hear what the
Colonel wrote to the mother of the dead soldier.' Then
they wrote the mother's thoughts, pulled her out of the
framework of the action after the gesture, 'she half-looked
up', and had her speak her feelings to the audience.

But the words they wrote for the mother still didn't
work. They were very sentimental and hysterical and un-
controlled, and came across like something out of a
women's magazine. We talked about whether or not it was
possible to communicate direct feelings of this kind.

I played them some Bessie Smith. And the next week
someone brought in a guitar, and tried to structure the
mother's feelings into a twelve-bar blues.

The work had been sustained over a number of weeks.
It had taken us from a discussion about a poem into an
involvement with different forms of theatre, a study of a
scene by Brecht, some analysis of film, some experience of
jazz, and some examination of the way people from differ-

ent social classes try to behave, and how this affects the art forms they produce. And all these subjects had been approached, not because they were down on a syllabus, which had to be covered, but because they were thrown up by physical work on a practical problem.

I was eager to push the work towards a final product. But the group only met on Friday mornings, and it was difficult to keep up the involvement beyond a certain point. In other projects I tried to run over a number of weeks, I found a similar pattern. Involvement rose steadily until about the fourth or fifth week, and after that the work began to take on the feel of something that had, unfortunately, to be finished.

We never finished the work on the poem. But these apparently 'non-academic' students had shown willingness and an ability to come to grips with ideas of some complexity, once they had become physically and imaginatively involved.

5

But I still believed that it was my real job to teach my subject: film. And so, I began inventing ways of getting students involved with finished bits of celluloid.

With a pre-diploma group, I 'made' a film about a fairground. We had no camera and no film: but they divided into small groups to produce a simple shooting script. I asked them to invent the first ten shots in detail, and then list a number of other things they would want to show in the film. The first suggestions of what they wanted to show included 'enjoyment', 'happiness', 'fun'. I asked them to find concrete images for these abstractions.

Several groups came up with the same idea for the opening sequence. The film would open with a long-shot taken from the top of a hill. In the distance, you would see the lights and the big wheel, and hear the music. Then a child would be seen skipping along a pavement with a wall behind. The camera would follow the child and then move round to show the entrance, followed by a close-up of the name of the fairground.

After we'd worked together on this script, I screened a
short film by Lindsay Anderson about the funfair in
Margate — *O Dreamland*. The film opens, unexpectedly,
with a shot of a uniformed chauffeur cleaning a Bentley
in a back alley, and only then cuts to a shot of people
going into the fairground.

I'd shown this film to many groups and tried to involve
them in discussion about this opening shot. Often, nobody
remembered having seen the shot. Most viewers certainly
attached little significance to the image — which is, of
course, a comment about the film's failure to communicate,
and not about the audience's lack of observation.

But in this case, the group was intrigued by the opening
shot. They were intrigued because they'd been working at
selecting an opening shot of their own. Why should a director choose something as unlikely as a shot of a Bentley for
the opening of a film about a fairground?

Clearly the director had selected the shot for a purpose.
The car was classy: but it was standing in a slum. And it
was in sharp contrast to the shoddy goods on offer inside
the fairground. The car, somebody suggested, belonged to
the owner of the fairground. Then the group went on to
discuss 'shoddiness'. 'Shoddiness' wasn't one of the abstractions they'd suggested. What concrete images represented
this abstraction?

The group looked at the film several times, and produced
some sharp analysis. They were willing to do so because
they'd been involved themselves at an inventive level. The
session was, for me, a step forward: but, looking back, I
can see that instinctively I assumed that the 'educational'
content lay in the analysis of Lindsay Anderson's finished
art object, rather than in the process of invention.

Another group turned a sequence from John Ford's
western *My Darling Clementine* into a collective comic
strip. This meant inventing a primitive language, with different hats for the hero and the villain. Again, what mattered to me was the analysis of the conventions involved,
not the quality of the comic strip. (A few years later,
students were making their own comic books with Tony
Earnshaw, who had invented *Wokker*, which ran for a year

in *The Times Educational Supplement* but proved to be
too philosophical for the readers.)

Yet another group transposed the closing stages of
Stanley Kubrick's film, *Paths of Glory*, into a radio tape.
The film is about the execution of French soldiers in the
First World War who have failed in an impossible attack
ordered by cynical generals who are manoeuvring for pro-
motion. The final sequence includes a jump-cut from the
execution to the generals having breakfast in a château. The
group worked for a long time at capturing the effect of this
visual cut in sound. The sequence also includes a long, im-
passioned diatribe by Kirk Douglas, which carries audiences
away on a first viewing, but which doesn't stand up to scrutiny. What delighted me particularly about the radio tape
was that when a student spoke, very accurately, but in a
Yorkshire accent, Douglas's words, the speech was alien-
ated in Brecht's sense of the word — that's to say, it
became possible to see clearly, from a cool point of view,
what the speech really meant. It was a technique we were
later to use in theatre group plays on the pronouncements
of politicians: but, again, at this stage, I was mainly concerned with the new dimension the exercise brought to the
film.

Eventually, I felt that the students *were* beginning to
look at films more closely. But I realised also that it was
only because I kept inventing trick ways of handling the
material. And I was quickly coming to the end of my
inventiveness.

I began to feel irritated with the students. It seemed to
me self-evident that a study of film was useful and desirable
for them. Why couldn't they see this? Why couldn't they
be *serious* about the work? Why did I constantly have to
think up new gimmicks to catch their interest? What did
they think I was — a conjuror drawing an endless supply of
rabbits out of a hat? Some kind of weekly entertainer?
Were those teachers in secondary schools, who wanted to
make film an examinable subject, right after all? Was that
the only way anybody could be persuaded to 'work'?

One afternoon, I caught myself acting like a schoolmaster again. I'd thought up yet another idea. We would

look at a film and pretend it was a piece of evidence in a
court case. The students would act as witnesses: they
would have to try and give an exact, detailed account of
what they had seen. They could be cross-questioned — and
in case of dispute, we could play back the film.

The idea worked so well that I decided to try it the following week. But by this time the students had caught on.
They came armed with note-books and began to copy
down a list of shots.

Suddenly, I had an image of myself years earlier teaching French to the lower stream of a small country grammar
school. None of those Norfolk boys saw any point in
learning French: I didn't see much point in teaching them
French. But that was what I was qualified to do and what
I was paid for. And it was on the timetable.

So we went through all the right rituals. I gave them
homework and most of them did it. I counted the exercise
books when they were handed in and pretended to make a
fuss about the ones that were missing. I gave them tests:
they ostentatiously stopped each other from copying. Then
they swopped papers, and marked each other's answers,
and argued about half-marks. And I wrote down the marks
in a big book, and totted up the positions each term.

We got on very well together. And every French period
we waited eagerly for the bell to go. Nobody learnt much
French.

And now, these art students and I were playing the same
meaningless game. Only instead of trying to memorise
French vocabulary, these students were trying to memorise the sequence of shots in the first ten minutes of
Renoir's *The Vanishing Corporal*. It seemed to me a particularly futile way of filling in an afternoon.

6

Why was I doing it?

It was easy to find any number of good, sound, intellec-
tually-convincing reasons. Film was a visual medium,
through which it was possible to teach 'discrimination'. Of
all the new media, it was the one which had produced

works most worthy of being compared to 'the great tradition' in literature. Film existed at the point where art met technology. It had created new physiological experiences, new ways of seeing. And it was also an industry. To analyse the structure of that industry and the way artists could operate in such a structure would be of direct relevance to art students who were themselves going to industrial jobs. It would have been simple to write out a highly respectable, academic syllabus arguing that a study of film would involve an approach to aesthetics, economics, perception, social psychology, sociology, history and several other disciplines. The value of the subject for art students was self-evident to me.

The trouble was that the value of any subject always seemed self-evident to the person teaching it. 'Why History of Art?', Nicholas Pevsner asked in an article in *Liberal Education* (January 1968); and he answered, 'History is a profitable thing to think about and work with for anybody. . . . If all history is worth diving into for all men, the history of art must be of twice the interest for all artists. . . and if a teacher of the history of art can't make his subject come to life for any group of students. . . that is his failure and not the failure of the subject.'

Again, such teachers as F.R. Leavis and Denys Thompson had argued that a literary education was 'more important than ever before; for in a world of this kind — and a world that changes so rapidly — it is on literary tradition that the office of maintaining continuity must rest.' The more extreme teachers saw the teaching of their subject as a kind of missionary activity. David Holbrook had written that the English teacher's subject 'must be at the centre of all education, the subject by which substance may be given to aims throughout.' English teachers were 'helping train the sensibility of three-quarters of the nation: and they are helping to create its capacities for living and its potentialities as an audience for new forms of popular culture.'

It now seems to me that such arguments stem from the teacher's assumption that because he is deeply involved with a particular subject, that subject must be of value and interest to everybody else. A man whose 'sensibilities' and 'capacities for living' have been largely shaped by reading books can only assume that people who don't share his commitment to literature will be in danger of having their responsiveness of feelings destroyed. So, a subject is placed at the 'centre of all education' — and a failure to make that subject 'come to life' becomes the teacher's failure.

I wasn't, in 1966, placing film at the 'centre of all education'. But I was discovering very sound reasons for arguing that, because I was interested in film, all my students should be as well. And in propounding these arguments, I was disguising the real reason why I was standing there, with that same group of students, every Wednesday afternoon.

The real reason why we were all there was that we, the students and I, were both products and working parts of an education industry. This industry had conditioned us to accept as normal a number of highly questionable assumptions. The most important of these assumptions were that education was something that took place in particular institutions; that, inside these institutions, pupils were organised into learning groups that would be administratively manageable; and that each learning group was to be handed over, at set times, to the care of a professional — an expert in an educationally acceptable subject — whose job it was to interest all the members of that particular group in his expertise.

The structure of the industry dictated the working relationship between teacher and students. If the working relationship was less than satisfactory — if the teacher failed to communicate his expertise to all the students — then there were two possible reasons. Either the students were particularly stupid; or the teacher was particularly inefficient.

Looking back over the whole of my experience of the education industry, as pupil and teacher, I could only conclude that the system was made up of stupid students and inefficient teachers. Unless, of course, there was something radically wrong with the assumptions on which the structure itself was based. And nobody seemed to be questioning the validity of the structure at all.

7

I tried to analyse what had happened to me, during my own formal education, as objectively as possible. I aimed at taking up the position Brecht advocated in *The Exception and the Rule:*

> Closely observe the behaviour of these people:
> Consider it strange, although familiar,
> Hard to explain, although the custom.
> Hard to accept, although no exception.
> Even the simplest action, apparently simple,
> Observe with mistrust. Check whether it is needed
> Especially if usual. . .

From a conventional point of view, I was one of the industry's successes. I'd won a scholarship at the age of ten and gone, from a working-class home, to a grammar school. I'd taken School Certificate at fourteen, spent four years in the sixth form, and ended up as head prefect. I'd won a state scholarship and gained common entrance to Balliol. At Oxford, I'd been awarded second class honours.

I totted up what I'd learnt during ten years at school and university. I spent six hours or more a week on the sciences for four years, and didn't learn enough to pass any of them at the very elementary School Certificate level. I did get a credit in maths: the teacher frightened me into it. But I couldn't now do the simplest quadratic equation. I learned a bit about geography: or at least about where places were. This was because I had war maps on my bedroom wall, and stuck pins in places as armies advanced and retreated. Since, while I was at school, mankind's principal occupation was to move armies around the globe, I learnt something about most of the world: but it wasn't what they taught and examined in geography. I scraped a School Certificate pass.

These were the subjects I was weak in — although at the time I was being frightened through maths, I was also school chess champion and could memorise whole games from chess books. But what really alarmed me about my analysis was how little I'd learned about the subjects in which I was supposed to be strong.

I was told I was good at languages. I learnt Spanish up to
School Certificate level (roughly the equivalent of O-level),
but could never really speak more than a few dozen sentences. Because of the war, there was nobody able to teach
me in the sixth form, so I let it drop. When I discovered I
needed Latin to get into Oxford, I learnt it in a year — but
could never remember any at all once I'd passed the exam.
This hindered me a lot at university, where I read French.
By the time I took my degree I could read and write French
tolerably well: but I only really learnt to speak with any
fluency several years later, when I worked in a camp in
France with French school kids.

I read French at Oxford because it never really occurred
to me to read anything else. It was one of my best subjects
at school — the only alternative, I thought, would have
been my other scholarship subject, English Literature —
but at Oxford at that time literature ended in the nineteenth century, and there was a lot of Anglo-Saxon. I was
just bright enough to avoid that: but nobody told me, (and
I only discovered it years later), that I'd been accepted at
Balliol because the Master, Lord Lindsay, had been interested in the political essays I'd written in the general paper.
He'd expected me to read Politics, Philosophy and
Economics: but I'd never done those subjects at school,
and never imagined I could have started them from scratch.
Nobody in the education industry put me wise.

My other main subject at school, besides French and
English, was history. I still have a vague, general sense of
history being divided into 'periods', European and English,
but can't remember in any real detail what happened in
these carved-out blocks of time. I've learned nearly all I
think I know about history long since I left school: but I
did quite well in the Higher School Certificate examination.

The reason why I did well in all my advanced subjects
was that what I really learned in the sixth form was how
to answer examination questions. There is, I suppose, a
certain value in being able to organise your smattering of
knowledge quickly and logically and express it concisely:
on the other hand, what happened for most of the time was
that I simply regurgitated other people's opinions, provi-

ded pat answers for what I was much later to recognise as complex questions, and expressed these opinions and answers in sentences made up of the right, received phrases together. There was no time to do anything else. To imagine that anybody can say something worthwhile about anything, while trying to answer five examination questions in three hours now seems to me to be absurd. But I was very good at it. (Years later, when I taught French in a country grammar school, I used the same answers on a class I'd entered for O-level French literature. I'd entered them because seventeen out of twenty-one of them had passed O-level language a year early, and the only way to keep them quiet was to offer them a way of winning an extra scrap of paper. We read the set texts in English, and for three periods of the week I dictated the right answers. For the rest of the time, we talked about football or cricket or the H-bomb. All twenty-one of them passed the examination, including the four who couldn't read the most elementary French.)

At Oxford, I used the answering techniques I'd learned at school to write weekly essays for my tutors. I can't remember writing any essay that contained any original thought or personal involvement until, three years after I'd taken my first degree, and after working for two years as a clerk in an office, instead of doing military service, I went back to Oxford to take a Dip.Ed., and became really engaged with the educational ideas of an authoritarian Catholic, Maritain.

Virtually nothing in the whole of my formal educational experience had ever connected with me in a way that involved me — me as a person. I had feelings, convictions, commitments to ideas and people. None of these seemed related to my 'work', which existed almost entirely on a verbal, argumentative level. I would discuss enthusiastically with my English teacher such questions as whether or not Hamlet was 'mad': but would never relate this to any experience I had of 'disturbed' people. And, although by the time I left school I thought of myself as something of a Marxist, I never used what little knowledge of Marxism I had to analyse, say, my own role in the school, or to help me decide what I should read at university. Everything existed for me in fragments.

I can, in fact, only remember one teacher at what was, in academic terms, a very successful school (six former pupils were in Balliol alone when I was — and there were many more in other Oxford or Cambridge colleges), who actually made connections for me. He came to teach art in my final year, and a group of us in the arts sixth were sent to him for one period a week. We didn't keep going for long. Not many of us were interested, and he didn't seem to think much of having to teach us. If he felt like it, he would bring a rugby ball out of a cupboard (we were a soccer school) and make us throw passes at each other round the art room. Most people never bothered to turn up.

He was the first teacher I met who ever talked about Freud; who drew any connections between Freud and Marx; and between them, and forms of art; who introduced me to surrealism, and to the links between surrealism and politics; who introduced me, too, to Herbert Read and his ideas of education through art; who had me reading hungrily essays on art and anarchy.

My fellow sixth-formers said this man was mad. He wasn't playing out his role as a teacher. Years later, I recognised his fellow in the teacher, in Vigo's film *Zéro de Conduite*, who behaves like Charlie Chaplin while he's on yard duty.

I never discussed these new discoveries with my own teachers. But they must have had some effect on my work in other subjects. The English master said I'd 'matured'. It was simply that, for the only time in my career at school and university, somebody had communicated with me on a level beyond that of the established education structure.

But it was to be a long time before I could find my own way out of that structure, into another, in which, for a few years at least, real education could begin to take place.

8

At school, and at university, I'd learnt to pass examinations. I hadn't needed to learn *why* to pass examinations. That

was made explicit, by my experience of social reality, both
at home and at school.

I was brought up in a working-class home in a Lancashire
cotton-town in the depression of the thirties. For as long
as I can remember, it was always assumed that I would 'get
on'. To 'get on' was to escape from the material limitations
of your background; to find for yourself some security in
a world that was insecure; to win for yourself some position
of influence, some degree of respect; to make yourself
financially comfortable. My father, a life-long socialist,
never questioned that I ought to 'get on', and that I would
'get on'. When my step-mother wanted me to leave school
after School Certificate and get 'a nice job in an office', he
never thought of agreeing. He had more ambition for me
than I had for myself.

At school, I was confronted by those who had 'got on'.
These were the teachers, who lived in a different world
from myself. They had 'got on' because they had passed
examinations: the gowns they wore in the classrooms, and
the resplendently coloured hoods they displayed on
Speech Days, were concrete demonstrations of their success. More important, passing examinations had made them
'experts' in a world too complicated for me to understand.
But what was clear was that they held the power in this
world. They controlled your lives. They could terrify you,
or make you laugh, or interest you, or bore you. But they
were the ones in command. They had privileges: while you
were sent out into the yard during the dinner-hour, they
sat in a staff room drinking tea. The history master might
explain to us the meaning of the word democracy, and
assure us that we lived in one. But our immediate experience taught us that the society in which *we* lived — the
school society — was organised by the people in power.
And they were in power because they'd succeeded in the
system; they'd won the bits of paper; they'd 'got on'.

I never once questioned, either at school or university,
the desirability of getting on. At school, you showed you
were getting on by becoming a prefect. That gave you a
glimpse of the power and the privileges. University was the
next rung of the ladder. You came out of Oxford one of

the controllers, instead of one of the controlled. The passport to this position of authority was your 'expertise'.

After I finally left Oxford, I went to teach. And, since a grammar school had given me my passport, I went to a grammar school. It was, I argued, very democratic: it gave opportunities to people like myself.

I taught in the grammar school for six years. I taught largely in the way I'd been taught myself. And since, in accepted terms, I'd been taught well, my teaching was acceptable. I got good examination results.

But in all the years I taught there, all my real involvements were outside. I played cricket for the town and chess for the county; published stories and tried to write a novel; got mixed up with CND; played the piano for a blues singer in a pub; put on a play.

Sometimes, the world of the school and the world of my personal involvements did begin to overlap. I ran a series of general studies classes with the sixth form, in which I talked about whatever happened to be interesting me — television, jazz, *Look Back in Anger*. A few of the students shared the same interests: our council house became the centre of an informal group of people who liked to meet and talk together.

But the structure imposed by the school dominated my working life. Which was how I came to find myself in that classroom, waiting for the bell. No matter how many working relationships I was able to create for myself outside the school structure, my main job was still to teach artificially-grouped classes English and French, according to a syllabus that had been laid down by other people; to keep order in my classroom; to get people through examinations; to play out, in short, the role of a schoolmaster. I'd 'got on'; but, in the process, I'd discovered that those who seemed to be in power were themselves trapped by the structure they were helping to maintain.

My own way out of the trap had come almost by chance. I'd published a few, not very good, short stories. On the strength of this, I was invited to run a Workers Education Association course. I enjoyed doing it, and later ran courses on drama and Dickens. Then I suggested a course on the mass media. This was considered very novel at the time. The course was a great success.

And, as a result of that, I'd become a full-time adult education tutor in Shropshire, where the authorities had left me free to develop my own courses, as long as I could find people to work with me. That was how the film work had developed. People had come to the classes, not because they were on a syllabus, or in order to win tickets which would help them 'get on', but because they were interested. And because, as we'd worked, we discovered new areas of common interest which we were eager to explore.

It had been a completely new educational experience for me. And it left me dissatisfied with a situation at Bradford in which the working relationships were again being limited by an administrative structure.

The students and I stared together at Jean Renoir on Wednesday afternoons. It was their job to try and be interested, whether they really were or not. And it was my job to find yet another way of 'bringing the subject to life'. And I'd run out of ways.

I'd been caught in a paradoxical situation. To me, liberal studies meant opening up possibilities, helping people to reach some awareness that they could control their own lives, change their own environment. But to both students and myself, liberal studies at Bradford had become a slot in the timetable. Like me, the students had learnt, by experience, from the age of five upwards, that they must expect their lives to be organised by 'them' — the people who'd 'got on', who told them what they should learn, arranged the timetables. And now, in my class, in an art college, the normality of this was being confirmed.

And I was helping to confirm it.

9

The irony is that while I was trying so unsuccessfully at Bradford to interest students in my 'subject', I was involved in a working relationship of a completely different kind with a group of students from Shrewsbury.

The students belonged to a theatre group, which we'd

formed almost accidentally the previous year. I'd been
asked to put on in Shrewsbury a short play by John Arden
and Margaretta D'Arcy, *Ars Longa, Vita Brevis*, and I
wanted to get away from the clichés of the amateur theatre
by working with people who had no preconceived ideas
about what theatre should be like. I was doing a weekly
class at Shrewsbury Art School at the time, and I simply
invited anyone who was interested to come along one
Saturday morning. About eight people turned up.

Ars Longa, Vita Brevis is set in a school. It tells the story
of an art master, whose passion for straight lines leads him
to turn an art class into a military exercise. In the end, he
finds his true role in the territorial army. He goes out on
Sunday manoeuvres and is shot by his headmaster, who is
out hunting with the governors. After his death, his widow
'enjoys herself with young men in fast cars'. She speaks his
epitaph:

> I shed a tear
> Upon his bier
> Because to me
> He was so dear
> But I could not follow him in all his wishes.
> I prefer the easy swimming of the fishes,
> Who sport and play
> In cool water all day
> And have not a straight line in the whole of their bodies.

John Arden and Margaretta D'Arcy had built the play
from children's games. And it was with children's games
that we started rehearsals.

At first, I was hesitant about asking young adults to play
like children. I didn't know how to begin. I had taken a
big ball along and we began to throw it to each other. We
formed a circle with a boy in the middle and tried to hit
him with the ball.

It took about twenty minutes for people to lose their
self-consciousness. Suddenly, we were all playing. Everybody began to remember games from childhood — blind
man's buff, British bulldog, Chinese lamp-posts, all kinds
of tigging and chasing games. We argued about the rules,

swapped technical terms with each other. We went berserk. It wasn't at all like those evenings in youth clubs when somebody suggests party games, and everybody shuffles self-consciously around. We really played, and after six hours we were covered with scratches and bruises. Then we sat round a tape-recorder and played games with words.

We went on playing for five or six sessions. At first the sense of physical release was exciting in itself — we were using our bodies in a way we had none of us used them for a long time. But, gradually, some of the games began to develop a dramatic pattern.

There was one game, for example, which was based on the idea of trying to move without being seen behind some-one's back. The person who was 'it' faced the wall; you tried to creep up on him; he turned round at unexpected moments; if he caught you moving, he sent you back to the beginning.

We turned this into a classroom scene. The person who was 'it' faced the blackboard and gave a lesson. The aim of the 'children' was to change places with each other without being caught. If you were caught, you became the teacher and carried on with the lesson.

One morning — during a liberal studies 'music' class in Shrewsbury — two of the girls made masks. They made a huge, crude cardboard mask, tied with string and crudely painted, for the art master. For the children, they produced bare, oblong bits of cardboard, with holes cut in them to see through. The bits of cardboard, unpainted, were just big enough to cover the eyes, and made everybody look disturbingly alike. The effect of six pairs of eyes, all turned towards the one teacher, was very un-nerving.

The art master carried huge cardboard boxes — squares and cubes and triangles. He tried to arrange them into a pattern for the 'children' to draw. The boxes kept falling down. Every time he turned his back to re-arrange the boxes, the 'children' changed position, leaving always one empty chair — a different chair each time. Whenever the art master turned to face the class, everybody froze. The bird-like eyes stared, unmoving, from behind the masks.

At a first reading, the Arden/D'Arcy scene was about an

authoritarian master, who is confronted by the natural
anarchy of children. But the game we had played had unearthed several levels of paradox. Behind the masks, the
children became a well-drilled, subversive, and slightly cruel
army. The art master, the authoritarian believer in straight
lines, became a man trying to cling to some sense of reality.
At the end of our scene, when, having set up a battle, he
stood on a chair conducting it, and shouting, 'Kill, kill, kill,
kill. . .', the bird-eyed children, instead of playing at killing
each other, suddenly turned on him. The scene remained
very funny, but became, also, a direct and powerful image
of the violence implicit in a classroom situation. And we
had arrived at this physical image by playing a children's
game.

The whole performance had about it this playful but
strongly physical quality. To the grotesque masks — we had
made one for each of the main characters — we added exaggerated costumes — old military red-coats, long black morning jackets, a fireman's helmet, a naval jacket. We borrowed
these from a local dramatic society: but there was no
'costume designer'. People invented their own physical
appearance, and the characters emerged from games,
costumes, masks.

We first presented the play in a normal theatre situation
for the Shrewsbury Theatre Guild. But later we played it
in all kinds of different situations — in schoolrooms, adult
education centres, in the open air at a Yorkshire village
festival (organised by John Fox, who was later to come to
Bradford and create The Welfare State); and most successfully of all, in a Bradford pub, as part of an evening involving Brian Patten reading his poetry, a local comedian, and
a pop group. (At the end of the evening, somebody said,
'If liberal studies were always like this, there wouldn't be
any trouble about attracting students'.)

After *Ars Longa Vita Brevis*, most of us wanted to keep
on working together. We went over to Ireland in the sum-
mer, and worked for a week with John Arden and
Margaretta D'Arcy on the creation of another short play,
Friday's Hiding. Back in Shrewsbury, we worked every
Sunday. We worked anywhere, in student flats, a room

over a pub, once in a garage attached to a semi-detached
house on the ring road. We had no facilities, no equipment,
and no money. For props we used cardboard boxes, beer
bottles, bits of wood, parts from old motor cars, anything
that happened to be lying around. For costumes, we used
sheets and blankets, coal scuttles and old clothes we picked
up in junk shops. We improvised from Boccaccio stories,
and re-wrote a script by Cervantes. But eventually we came
back to Arden/D'Arcy, and put on a full-length production
of *The Happy Haven*.

The Happy Haven grew up as a collective invention, and
set a pattern for much of the work that was to follow at
Bradford. Nobody appointed a dress designer, or a set
designer, or a lighting director. One student, Frank
Challenger, went off and made a set of masks. Another
learnt how to set the lights. All of them collected their own
costumes, wearing old people's things over black jeans, so
that throughout they were obviously young people playing
at being old. In rehearsal, Arden himself stressed that the
comedy had to be fast and manic, and that they had to
move quickly, only making 'old' gestures when they
wanted to show precisely how old people moved and be-
haved. And so the performance was full of movement: one
character did an enormous leap from a high stage, shouting,
'Because we're *old*'.

The students put their own set together from the
materials to hand. They used white exhibition screens to
shut off the corners of the stage, and built a high upper
stage by laying planks across stacked tables. They made
their own props, including a huge cardboard cut-out birthday cake, and a cardboard cut-out decanter in which yellow
liquid turned green: one side was painted yellow, the other
green, and the fake conjuring trick was made ludicrously
obvious. They created a night scene without using lighting,
simply by putting nightshirts over their jeans and carrying
candles. They worked on the script in pairs. Each pair
would begin by improvising a scene and work gradually
towards the written text whilst creating music-hall routines.
Then they would show the results to the rest of the group,
who offered criticism and advice. Towards the end, all I

had to do was organise the more complicated group scenes.
At the very last moment, at Margaretta D'Arcy's suggestion,
we introduced a piano, which accompanied the action with
music-hall tunes. The final production must, by conventional standards, have been crude. But it had energy, directness, freshness — and, above all, it was *funny*. (Arden's
plays had often, it seemed to me, been killed by humour-
less productions.)

The Happy Haven was the most sustained piece of work
we'd done until then; and it was satisfying in a way that
seemed to be impossible in formal, institutionalised
situations.

Moreover, it was the most 'educational' work I'd ever
been involved in. Even from an academic point of view
we'd learnt a lot about a 'subject' — modern drama. Ideas
that the theatre establishment had boggled at — such as,
that it was possible to *show* old people while playing in a
young, active way — the students had taken in their stride.
We had talked all around Arden's ideas, explored the connections between the political content and the style,
related Arden to other forms of theatre, to pantomime
and music-hall, and related these forms to Shakespearian
popular conventions. We had discussed all these things, not
because we were studying 'theatre history', but because of
the working context. We explored theory when there were
practical problems to solve.

Again, we had been developing an understanding of the
way language could be handled. We had moved through
scenes improvised around general ideas to the precise words
Arden had set down. We had reached these words, not out
of any literary respect for a text, but because we had discovered that Arden could say more in his words than we
could by using ours. We had come to grips with what
educationalists call 'the use of English' in a direct, concrete
way.

Again, we'd been learning about communication — by
communicating, first, with each other, and then with audiences. We'd been learning how to make analytical judgements by constantly questioning our own inventions: the
mythical gap between invention and criticism had been

bridged. We'd even been learning simple acting techniques:
how to time a gesture or a movement to make people
laugh.

But perhaps what we'd learnt above all was how to
create our own working situation, and how to manage it.
As the work developed, we all became aware that through
our own actions we were extending our possibilities. All
of us began to get a sense that what we did depended on
us — and not on a structure that had been set up by a group
of administrators.   ⌐→ of words?

At Shrewsbury, we felt free to make our own working
situation. In Bradford, I felt as trapped as the students who
were officially compelled to attend my classes.

I decided to leave Bradford. But before I did, a colleague,
Bill Gainham, suggested that I should try a different way
of working with a group of his students. Why, he argued,
did we have to submit to someone else's structure? Why
not work the other way round — ask ourselves what condi-
tions we needed, and set about getting them?

The conversation led to the setting up of the first complementary studies project at Bradford, and to the staging
of the first event. And so, indirectly, to the work that was
to be produced in the next few years.

10

Bill Gainham was the director of the printed textiles course.
He was a graduate in textiles from Leeds University, but
while he was there he had been involved with a lot of other
activities, including the editing of a film magazine, *Scope*,
which he had turned into one of the sharpest instruments
of film criticism in the country. Later, he had taught for a
while in a secondary modern school. He had been invited
to give one lesson in English. He had gone into the classroom for the first period in the afternoon and announced
that he was from the Ministry of Food and had come to
investigate complaints about school dinners. Each boy
would be allowed to make a complaint in one sentence. In
turn. After each complaint, he provided an answer. 'School
dinners are lousy,' a kid would say; and he would reply,

'The quality of these meals has been measured and attested by our experts and found to be highly satisfactory. Next.' As the lesson went by, the criticisms had grown more specific. By the end of the period, several boys in the class were threatening to bring sandwiches. Nobody asked Bill Gainham to take any more English lessons.

Bill Gainham rejected totally the idea that, because the college had failed to get Dip.A.D. and was now 'vocational', we were committed to a lower level of education. He rejected, too, the notion of a difference between 'education' and 'training'. 'Why,' he was to write a letter to *New Society*, 'why is it so hard in England to connect education with the boots on our feet as well as the caps on our head?' To him, a good curtain design meant the successful carrying out of ideas. The more ideas a student could command, the more effective he would be as a craftsman. 'We do not believe,' we later wrote, 'that there are two kinds of people — the "purposive designers", who have problems to solve, and the bohemians who "learn through enjoying themselves". What we are seeking is a working method that is *generally applicable* in education.'

Before I arrived in Bradford, Bill Gainham had organised, as part of his printed textiles course, a week's project on the 1930s. His students had looked at thirties designs, seen thirties films, played thirties songs, read George Orwell, listened to Philip Toynbee. He now suggested that we should try out a pilot scheme with a similar group. We would offer a five-day project. Only those students who wanted to take part in it need do so: but those who did join the project would be released from any other commitments for the whole week. The aim of the project was to turn a simple game into a complex, but self-explanatory, dramatic event.

We put the suggestion to a group of second-year students, who had been working with me for one morning a week, and most of them were eager to take part. We took over a bare, dusty room on the ground floor of a mill that had been turned into a college annexe. The room was completely bare, but with a large, raised platform running across one end. This formed a natural stage — there was even a door, which could be used as an entrance, in the back wall. On the back wall, too, there was a box containing the light switches: the room was lit by fluorescent tubes. There was no air in the room, and the rest of the ground floor was taken up by technical college students working on very noisy machines. We could only actually rehearse when they weren't there — which meant working lunch-times and in the evenings.

We began with a blindfold game. It's one I've used very often since then, and it's very good, both to play and to watch. In the playing area, a slipper is placed. Two players have blindfolds. The first player is looking for the slipper: the second player is looking for the first player. The game ends, either when the first player finds the slipper, or is caught by the second player.

When the game is played on a stage, dramatic patterns develop. The players form spatial relationships with each other. As they move towards each other, the tension is built up. Or the game becomes funny, with players blundering past each other and never meeting. It's important for the spectators to keep silent and still, otherwise the tension is broken. The game becomes more complicated when four players are introduced, working in pairs.

We played this game until the players became very skilful. They would sit silent for a long time, or would throw objects to make distracting sounds. Soon, they could find their way around the stage without difficulty, and so, to add to the interest, the group made a mobile structure, which hung down from cross-beams, which, in turn, hung down from the ceiling, but which swung freely on the end of a rope. If anybody collided with any of the objects hanging down from the cross-beams, the whole contraption spun round. The objects included a sack, stuffed, like a body; a pink polythene bag; balloons; lots of old junk; and tin cans filled with stones and pebbles. As the mobile whirled round, the stones and pebbles made an accidental and completely random rhythm.

This set was completely functional: but it also looked very strange and interesting. And it became even more surprising when a boy discovered that by flicking the switches in the box at the back of the stage, he could make the fluorescent lighting travel up and down the room to produce after-images. The after-images were heightened when, instead of wearing scarves, the players put tall, stiff potato bags over their heads. They became strange, alien creatures. To the lighting was added a high-pitched shriek, produced by feed-back put through two amplifiers belonging to one of the students who worked with a pop group. When the lights flashed and the amplifiers shrieked, both eyes and ears were being bombarded (this was two years before the 'light shows' and 'psychedelia').

Gradually, we put a story together. It was a story completely without words, and was intended to be self-explanatory. During the week, we kept inviting people in to watch, and to describe what they saw. If there was anything not clear, we changed it.

The story opened with the stage in darkness. Only vague shapes could be seen. A drum began to beat slowly. Subdued sounds came through the amplifier. Suddenly, a light flashed, illuminating a structure, a number of figures with paper bags for heads, a boy with a drum, and a girl in black bra and pants, sitting on a chair reading a magazine. Presently, the lights flashed more and more quickly, the sound built up to a shriek, the girl began to scream. When the lights and sound reached a climax, a referee's whistle was blown. The noise stopped, and all the lights came up.

On the stage were the drummer, the girl, the referee, five players — and a boy in a raincoat, who worked the lights. The referee wore a black bowler hat, a black frock coat and pin-striped trousers, all of which were too big. The players had paper bags over their heads. Two carried blue flags and two carried red. The fifth player had a blue flag: but he also carried a stick with the stars and stripes wrapped round it. This boy was the killer. At either side of the stage were balloons, five red at one side, five blue at the other.

The referee blew his whistle, and the players began to move. The killer was looking for the people with red flags, to kill them: but when he caught anybody, he never knew whether the flag was red or blue. He killed them all just in case.

He announced the decision to kill by raising his stick in the air. At this, the referee blew his whistle, and everybody froze. The referee led the victim to the front of the stage. The stage went black, lights flashed, the amplifiers shrieked, the girl screamed. When the lights went on again, the victim would be lying at the front of the stage, still clutching his flag. His place had been taken by another player, shoved in through the door at the back. The referee burst a balloon, red or blue as the case may be, blew his whistle, and the game re-started.

When the referee decided that enough people had been killed, he blew for full-time. He led all the remaining players to the front of the stage, raised the dead, and put everyone in line. Then he counted the balloons to see which side had won. The winners were given medals: they consisted of cog wheels, carried, on a tray covered by a velvet cloth, by the boy who worked the lights. The losers had their flags taken away. Then the boy who worked the lights handed the referee a guitar-case, and placed a black scarf over the referee's eyes. Using his guitar, the referee shot the lot, winners and losers alike. They fell in a heap. The referee used the black scarf as a duster to clean his guitar; put the guitar back in its case, and left through the audience. The boy who had done the lighting went round the dead bodies, stealing watches, wallets, rings, money, and putting them in his raincoat pocket.

When John Arden saw it, he said the plot never developed. So we invented a half-time, during which the dead bodies sat up and played cards. Since none of them could see, they played in different directions. They tried to hide their cards from each other. The referee played, and looked at everybody's hand. He collected all the winnings.

We called the event *Performance.* In the college community, it was a great success. A lot of students came and saw it and enjoyed it — and also stayed to play the game themselves.

I tried to analyse what the students had learnt during the work. They'd learnt something about their bodies — how to move without eyes, how to keep completely still when everything is moving all around. The girl who'd sat reading the magazine throughout had, in particular, learnt how to control her body in this way, how to be totally concentrated.

They'd learnt how to invent a game that would be self-explanatory. This was, in fact, an astringent intellectual exercise. It had involved at each step checking and re-checking, consulting with onlookers, trying to see what was happening in objective terms.

And they'd learnt something about communicating with audiences, about varying the rhythms in such a way as to maintain the interest, about making people laugh.

But for me the real success of the event lay in the fact that, inside an educational institution, it had been possible to create a situation in which people could work freely together, bringing their individual skills to a collective situation, not because it was part of a syllabus, but because that was what they wanted to do.

The real question was whether this was an isolated situation that couldn't be repeated: or whether it was possible to make the creation of such situations the centre of an educational structure.

I decided, before I left Bradford, to try, with Bill Gainham, to work out a practical structure. I began the work as a farewell exercise. But by the time it was finished, I'd made up my mind that, for the next few years, this was the structure in which I wanted to work.

10

There were, as I saw it, three main problems.

First: compulsory liberal studies seemed to me to be a contradiction in terms. Complementary studies only existed at the moment because the D.E.S. and Coldstream said they had to exist. Until the students themselves felt they *wanted* to be involved, complementary studies, however nominally liberating, would continue to be an authoritarian imposition dictated by administrators.

Secondly: it was unreasonable to expect all the students in a particular group to *want* to involve themselves in the same liberal studies subject. Students, at the moment, came to complementary studies together, not out of common interest, but because they happened to be 'textiles' students or 'graphics' students. In other words, they were grouped, in complementary studies, not according to interest or commitment, but because they came from a particular department. They were grouped for administrative convenience.

Thirdly: the limits of their involvement were at present set by a weekly timetable. The *Performance* event had demonstrated that, over a few days, it was possible to generate a lot of energy. Such an escape from the timetable seemed to me essential.

The key to the structure, then, lay in offering all the students as free and open a choice as possible; in enabling students from different departments to come together on a basis of common interest; and in making it possible for them to work together long enough to allow energy to be released and commitment to be developed.

And we had to be able to convince other people that it was workable.

In the end, the proposal I made was that we should ask every full-time student in college to do one complementary studies project a year. Each project would last for two weeks, during which the students would be released completely from all departmental requirements. At the beginning of each year, we would offer as wide a range of projects as possible, and we would offer them right across the board to all the students. All the students would be free to decide which project they wanted to join. Departmental tutors would be asked to give priority to the student's express wishes.

The important point was the scale of the proposal. There were between 250 and 300 students in college. If we offered thirty projects, it was reasonable to hope that everybody in college would find at least one of them interesting. I added that if any students really didn't like any of the projects, they should be free to come to me and discuss what they might do.

I expected to meet a lot of opposition from the other departments. The scheme meant that there would always be one or two students missing from each department. In fact, everybody was philosophical. At least, the work of the departments wouldn't be disrupted for one afternoon a week: and most people recognised that there were always one or two students missing, through sickness and other reasons, without the departments falling to pieces. And, since the programme was to be offered at the beginning of the year, they would know when to expect students to be missing, and be able to plan accordingly.

What, I am sure, influenced the attitude of the Principal, who strongly supported the proposal, was the knowledge that, with the failure of the Dip.A.D. application, Bradford had little to offer. Any distinctive idea was better than none. If an experiment in an alternative structure of education could keep the college independent, then it was worth trying.

And so, much to my surprise, the proposal was accepted, and immediately after *Performance* we were able to begin planning a radical new programme.

Chapter two
Towards a cheerful
and militant learning

'It is in fact nothing short of a miracle that the modern
methods of instruction have not yet entirely strangled the
holy curiosity of enquiry . . . . I believe it would be possible
to rob even a healthy beast of prey of its voraciousness if
it were possible, with the aid of a whip, to force the beast
to devour continuously, even when not hungry.'

Albert Einstein

'Generally there is felt to be a very sharp distinction
between learning and amusing oneself. The first may be
useful, but only the second is pleasant. Well, all that can be
said is that the contrast between learning and amusing oneself is not laid down by divine rule; it is not one that always
was and must continue to be . . . . there is such a thing as
pleasurable learning, cheerful and militant learning.'

Bertolt Brecht, *Theatre for Pleasure and Theatre
for Instruction*

1

I had spent a year in Bradford reaching towards an educational structure inside which students and teachers could
come together freely to work on projects of common
interest. The structure was now there. The immediate problem was how, in a matter of weeks, to put together a programme which would give life to the idea.

Theoretically, we could have gone round the students
asking them what they wanted to do. But there was no
time for this if we were to get the scheme off the ground:
and I rejected the idea, too, for educational reasons.

The aim was to break out of the straitjackets which subject barriers had imposed on both teachers and students. But the idea of a breakout was important. And until the students had been placed in the position of seeing and experiencing the possibilities, they, as well as the teachers, were limited by their own preconceptions.

To begin by asking students what they wanted to do was already to define the limits, in the way that television producers define limits when they talk of 'giving people what they want'. People can only know what they want when they know what's available. I saw it as my job to offer the full range of the possibilities that were available to me at that time.

In practice, I built the first programme around people. I thought of anybody I'd ever heard of who'd done exciting and imaginative work with people. Then I contacted as many as possible and asked them what they would like to offer a group of fifteen students for a fortnight. I encouraged them not to think up 'popular' projects, but to start from ideas that interested and even obsessed *them*, ideas that under other circumstances they had never been able to put into practice. Within a few months, I'd been able to put a programme together that included a Professor of International Politics, Laurence Martin, who was willing to play a war game; a National Theatre director, Geoffrey Reeves, who agreed to take part in a theatre workshop; and a popular poet, Adrian Mitchell.

I was able to pay for these and other visiting teachers because, by complete coincidence, the full-time art historian was leaving to go to the United States. Instead of replacing her, I used her salary to bring in these outsiders.

Anybody looking through that first year's programme would find a great deal of variety, but would have to look more closely to discover a common education thread. Some of the projects were obviously 'relevant' to students — particularly two offered by a young lecturer, Stephen Brook, who had worked with Richard Hoggart in Birmingham, but who lived in Halifax. He directed projects on *A Halifax Beat Club*, and *Teenage Clothes*. But other projects — including one I put forward on *Hot Gospel*, simply because I was fascinated by the pentecostals, amongst

whom I'd been brought up — seemed a long way away
from student concerns. There were projects directly connected with practical activities — *Theatre Workshop*,
Making a Film, *Making a Radio Ballad*. There were others
— *Living in a Village*, *Bradford in 1910* — which were
conventionally environmental.

I argued at the time that it was possible to define a
number of precise educational aims that were common to
all the projects, and that were based on what we imagined
student needs to be. So, we wanted to help students communicate more lucidly, with each other, with their tutors,
and with their future employers and colleagues. We felt
that they needed to understand what working with people
in a concrete situation meant; to know how to persuade
other people to accept their ideas; to realise that they were
not helpless cogs in a wheel, but that situations were
changeable, and that they could act as agents of change.
We wanted to teach them how to acquire facts, and how to
make judgements about the facts they acquired. Above all,
we wanted them to be able to look, in a cool, questioning
way at themselves, and at things they took for granted
about the world they lived in.

All these were good, solid, respectable, educational
aims: but years later we found that they could be shared
by people who did not share our way of working. And it
was this way of working that formed the real thread running through our programme.

The way of working involved, in the widest sense of the
term, education through theatre. Not theatre in the sense
of putting on plays, although this later became a part of it,
but theatre in the sense of setting up concrete situations
through which people could learn, directly and by experience, how to handle and use concepts that, in the abstract,
had seemed complex and mystifying. Brecht used to have
a card over his desk which read, 'Truth is Concrete'. We
tried to invent situations that would turn abstract ideas
into concrete experiences.

The situations themselves formed the centre of the
learning process. For example, at one stage we set up a project called *Christie in Halifax*. Christie was the murderer

who'd strangled women in London. He'd been born in
Halifax and had lived there until after the First World War.
We chose to look at Halifax by way of Christie because that
provided a dramatic focus for an examination of, amongst
other topics, social history. The students wrote to the
newspapers and asked anyone who'd known Christie to
contact them. And a very old, very respectable lady, a
retired headmistress, did so. So they went to film her, and
when they got there she would talk about anything except
Christie. The content of the experience they had in filming her was not what she said about Halifax before the
First World War, but the fact that they found themselves
in a complex relationship with her. The encounter itself
told them more about social conventions, about how
people felt it was proper to behave, about how the manners
of previous decades shaped response to a present situation,
than anything they brought back on the tape. To me, this
was an example of learning through a dramatic situation.

The extent to which the projects in that first year's programme related to this concept of education through
theatre varied from project to project. But three projects
in particular turned out to be 'dramatic' in different ways.
They were Laurence Martin's *Vietnam War Game;* a project
I invented on *Hot Gospel;* and Adrian Mitchell's *Making
Poetry Public.* All three of them laid the foundations for
future work, and are therefore, worth examining in
some detail.

2

Ten students opted for the *Vietnam War Game*, they had
all met before the project began. They had attended six
weekly seminars on the Vietnam situation, in which they
had been presented with the background to the conflict.
The seminars were conventional in form: since the students
were gathering information that would help them in the
game they were interested in playing, they were quite
happy to get their information straight. The only theatre I
introduced at this stage consisted of my taking up particular positions and defending them. In one session, for

example, I spoke on behalf of the United States embassy, putting forward arguments that had been put to a group of us by the embassy when we had been working on Peter Brook's *US*.

During the first week of the project, we developed this background work. We studied books, magazines, propaganda films from both sides. We improvised some of the stories we read, often switching roles. For example, we divided into two groups. One group was a US army patrol, the other Vietnamese villagers. The patrol was questioning the villagers about the Vietcong. At a certain point, a signal was given, and the roles were reversed.

Towards the end of the week, the students chose the parts they were going to play in the game. A wealthy textile design student from Malaya, who was violently anti-communist, insisted on playing the current Saigon leader, Marshal Ky. An apprentice jeweller, a Polish emigré, who was also violently anti-communist, became President Johnson. An active member of the Young Conservatives cast himself as the Soviet Union. Two bright girl dress-designers made up the American delegation; two first-year boys played China and North Vietnam respectively; and a Buddhist and an NLF representative (a girl who never spoke for three days) completed the group. As soon as the groups had been formed, the students began daubing rival slogans around the college, much to the consternation of some members of the administration.

Laurence Martin gave the students a document to study two days before the game began. It described a rapidly developing crisis situation. The United States had bombed areas close to the Chinese frontier, and there were rumours of a threatened blockade of Haiphong. (Laurence Martin told me privately that such a move was inconceivable: the Americans would never behave in this way — but he thought this was a crisis the students would respond to. The move may have been inconceivable in 1966 when we played the game: but the blockade was, of course, actually carried out as part of the Nixon/Kissinger peace policy in 1972.)

The last statement on Laurence Martin's document read:

'3 February, 1967: *Washington* — A Defence Department spokesman announced that further reinforcements of destroyers and other types of escort vessel were being sent to the Seventh Fleet.'

The game was organised so that the group met every two hours to announce moves. The moves had to be put in writing and read out. But it was possible to hand secret moves to the umpires. The tutors acted as umpires. Their job was simply to prevent people making moves that were impossible. In very rare cases they might reject a move because of its implausibility.

Between the two-hourly meetings, the groups negotiated with each other. They wore badges of identity, and set up their headquarters in various rooms around the college. Their first move, in fact, was to negotiate with the tutors who controlled these rooms, and persuade the tutors to give them space for the game.

The game quickly developed its own impetus. To the rival slogans on the walls, rival news bulletins were added. And the personal involvement of the students began to lead to an awareness of problems usually ignored in political studies.

For example, personal feelings became tangled with political decisions: One of the 'US' girls and the 'Russian' boy strongly disliked each other. This made negotiations between the United States and the Soviet Union particularly tense — I thought about the stories of the relationship between Eden and Dulles at the time of Suez. The girl and the boy sat at opposite ends of the college pub, exchanging insults.

On the third day, the Polish boy playing President Johnson appeared in the umpires' office with tears of rage in his eyes. The girls, he said, were being unreasonable. They wouldn't let him drop an H-bomb on Peking. 'Nobody could ever stop President Johnson from acting according to his conscience,' he cried dramatically. He resigned and became General de Gaulle instead. When he was asked to put his resignation into writing, he produced, 'By resigning from the American delegation, I want to protest about the American policy in Vietnam and this is

the reason why I resigned from the American delegation.'
Later, however, he was to show a healthy cunning. He
handed in a dramatic move: 'Selling arms to Red China
without *any* obligation.' To the umpires, he handed in a
secret 'Reason for Move': 'Disused aircraft and guns,
which would have gone for scrap.' As de Gaulle, he enjoyed
freedom without responsibility: at every meeting, he laid
on the table denunciations of all concerned. Everybody
read them hurriedly then went on with the serious business
of negotiation.

As the week progressed, written contributions tended
to become more sophisticated. The North Vietnamese
poured out a torrent of propaganda: 'The people's will and
spirit cannot be measured, the spirit of the people cannot
be crushed.' The Soviet Union referred to 'a good-will visit
of naval vessels — three cruisers, seven destroyers and two
nuclear-powered submarines' to the port of Haiphong.
When the Chinese went back on a secret agreement they'd
made, the Russian delegation wrote: 'Once again, China
has left the burden of preventing American aggression
squarely on the shoulders of the Soviet Union and the
Democratic Republic of Vietnam.' The students learnt this
language from the wealth of pamphlets and news reports
which were constantly available.

Meanwhile things began to happen outside the conference room. The players had succeeded in establishing themselves in studios all over the college. The Chinese delegation, for example, was located in the middle of the
foundation-year painting studio. There, amongst the abstract exercises in colour, he sat at a desk beneath a portrait
of Chairman Mao and waited to be negotiated with. The
Americans had taken over a room above the jewelry workshop: delegates had to move through the jewelling apprentices to reach the US embassy. As players went from room
to room, negotiating with each other, students who
weren't actually in the game began to intervene.

Towards the end of the week, the news suddenly went
round that the Americans were about to blockade
Haiphong. The Americans had problems. They'd lost their
President, a Russian fleet was sailing towards Haiphong,

the Russians and Chinese had made some kind of agreement, the details of which remained secret, and the NLF had blown up the embassy in Saigon. At this moment, the two girls playing the US delegation came out of their room to find the stairs blocked by a group of students, sitting down and waving banners. The girls kicked their way angrily through the demonstration, which they accused me of having organised. 'Aren't we in enough trouble without this?' one of them said. The leader of the demonstration made himself Bertrand Russell. He studied Russell's contributions to the Cuban Missile Crisis, then wrote letters to the participants, congratulating the Russians on their restraint and hectoring the Americans. These were read out at the next conference meeting, and thrown away. At the end of the game, Russell issued a statement saying that once again he had saved the peace of the world.

The game reached a climax of mutual deception. It was virtually won by the girl playing the NLF, who hadn't spoken for the first few days. She had already made a startling contribution. Since the Saigon representative had refused to sit at the same negotiating table as the NLF, she'd suggested two tables, with Saigon at one, the NLF at the other, and everybody else at both. (This suggestion pre-dated by about two years the agonising discussions about tables during the Paris negotiations.) Now, as the Russians and Americans announced, with their final move, an agreement to call off the blockade, she produced a trump card. She'd been negotiating quietly with the Buddhists, and had agreed, temporarily, to work with them on paralysing Saigon with a general strike. The boy playing Ky resigned in angry protest because the umpires allowed the move. He said the NLF would never have any influence in Saigon. Two months later, the Tet offensive began.

All the people playing the great powers claimed to have won.

The game had been entertaining, but what had the students learnt? Well, they'd learnt something about Vietnam and international politics; and about the way politicians behave; and about how language can be manipulated for political purposes. In learning to handle language

unscrupulously themselves, they'd come to see through
some of the processes of mystification. But also, in working together, negotiating, finding solutions to specific
problems, they'd been developing, in a practical way, skills
they might later find useful in their jobs.

One aspect of the game only really struck us when it was
all over. We'd all become so involved in the immediate reality of the game situation that the wider realities — that,
as we played, there really was a war going on in Vietnam
tended to be forgotten. What we had, in fact, created for
ourselves was a concrete, dramatic image of the way in
which, in contemporary political life, the processes of the
power game can become divorced from any over-all social
or political reality. It was an experience Noam Chomsky
was later to analyse in *The Backroom Boys.*

In the end, what made the *Vietnam War Game* important
for future work were the dramatic possibilities we had discovered. If we had gone off to play the game by ourselves
in some country house — as Laurence Martin had previously done with his university students — we should, no
doubt, have still learnt something about international politics. But the fact that we played the game openly, all over
the college, using emblems, posters, wall-newspapers,
turned the simulation game into a piece of theatre in which
the audience — the college community — began to partici-
pate, quite spontaneously, and without being asked to do
so.

The event had a considerable effect on the college community for the week it lasted. I began to wonder what
effect a similar event might have if we staged it outside the
college, in the wider community of the city. And in this
way the *Vietnam War Game* led directly, the following
year, to our staging of the Russian Revolution in the streets
of Bradford.

3

Marching in chorus,
Jesus before us,
Foursquare Gospel workers are we;

> Though men may taunt us,
> Nothing can daunt us,
> On then to victory;
> Jesus the Saviour,
> Jesus the Healer,
> Baptizer, Coming King,
> Ever is near us,
> Ready to cheer us,
> On then, and let us sing.
>
> *Elim Chorus*

If the *Vietnam War Game* turned out to be theatrical in a way none of us had foreseen, the *Hot Gospel* project was dramatic in a different way. This time the drama arose from the coming together of two contrasting groups of people — art students and pentecostal believers.

The aim of the project was to find out what went on in pentecostal churches and mission-halls; to discover what pentecostals believed; and to examine how their beliefs affected the way they lived their lives. The methods included listening to talks and expositions by pentecostal leaders; attending and taking part in pentecostal meetings; and making tape-recordings of individual pentecostalists of all kinds and social classes, talking about their religious experiences. These tape-recordings were built around very simple, concrete questions. Starting from the four basic pentecostal beliefs (as expressed in the *Elim Chorus*), Salvation, Divine Healing, Baptism in the Holy Ghost, the Second Coming, we framed the questions in direct, personal terms: 'Have you ever been saved? When? What happened?' 'Have you ever had any experiences of miraculous healings?' 'Have you ever been "baptized in the Holy Ghost?" Can you describe exactly what it felt like?' 'Suppose Jesus were to come back to-morrow? What precisely do you imagine would happen?' During the whole project, we never entered into any theological arguments, simply asked questions and listened. Then we would bring back the tape-recordings and analyse them together. By way of comparison, we also talked, during the fortnight, to

seventh day adventists, Jehovah's witnesses and christian
scientists, and we made a long recording of a healer who
was a spiritualist medium. At the end of the project, we
played the tapes to a lecturer in psychology from the university and asked him to analyse them from his point of
view. We also listened to a highly entertaining lecture by
the university Reader in Biology, who talked about
'*Science as a Hot Gospel*'.

Twelve students from all departments of the college
took part. The element of dramatic confrontation began
on the first day when they encountered the leader of the
local apostolic church, a man called Pastor Weeks.

We had begun the project with a short, general discussion about what we were trying to achieve, and then the
students had divided themselves up into four or five groups
and gone out to look for pentecostal churches in Bradford.
The idea was that they would first have to discover for
themselves what churches could be covered by the blanket
word 'pentecostal'. They were asked to locate the churches,
make a list of the times of meetings, so that we could
plan visits; and, particularly, to write down any uses of language that might strike them as being unusual. (One group,
for example, returned with 'Breaking of Bread'.) Learning
the pentecostal language was to become a central part of
the project.

One of the groups discovered the apostolic church two
miles up the road from the College of Art. According to
one of the official histories of the pentecostal movement —
I'd collected together a good deal of literature about pentecostalism and left the books about the studio for reference
— the apostolic church was a breakaway group, which had
been formed in 1916. There were dark references in the
history to 'grave errors and extravagances' and to 'dangerous extremes', but the writer, Donal Gee, later comments,
'The passage of years has modified extremes in all parties,
and, with others, the apostolic church has learned by some
of its mistakes'. Compared with another group the students
were later to encounter, the apostolic church in Bradford
was a centre of dignified respectability. This was certainly
true of Pastor Weeks himself, who, in all his dealings with

the students, went out of his way to reveal himself as an
intelligent, rational, but above all, *common-sense* person.
Whenever, for example, he said anything that he thought
might be unacceptable from this common-sense point of
view, he would always introduce it with such phrases as,
'You may not, of course, accept this', or 'I do sincerely
believe. . .'.

The students had met him in the apostolic church book-
shop. We had, that afternoon, planned to look at a film
about a pentecostal church in Manchester (Denis Mitchell's
TV film *Sharon*). The students invited him to see the film
with us and to talk about it afterwards.

I'd borrowed *Sharon* because I thought it was a particularly good example of the way I hoped the students would
work. Denis Mitchell's great quality — as a maker of both
radio and television programmes — lies in his ability to
listen, with genuine interest, to the people he's working
with. Most media interviewers take up strong, preconceived
positions. They ask their questions with a brash certainty
that they already know the answers: 'So you saw a flying
saucer at the bottom of your garden? What. . .' (with a
knowing glance at the camera) 'what did it look like?
You're sure it couldn't have been something else? Do you
often see things that don't exist. . .?' Mitchell's approach
is to assume that people have something valid and interesting to say, and to encourage them, as unobtrusively as
possible, to say it, without interposing his own preconceptions.

Sharon consists of a number of sequences filmed during
healing meetings at Sharon tabernacle, an old chapel set in
a Manchester slum, intercut with short, personal statements made direct to camera. Two pastors pray for the
sick by laying hands on them. Some of those prayed over
fall to the floor. A woman who says she hasn't walked for
years limps slowly, but with increasing confidence, round
the room, the camera following her feet through the first
tentative steps. Another woman begins to move forward
for healing, but before she can say what is wrong with her,
one of the pastors says the Lord has told him that she has
a pain in her back and that she's been healed. 'Touch your

toes', he says, and she does so in amazement. Later, a woman playing a piano very badly, leads a group of children, including a number of cheerfully bewildered West Indians, through a song called 'Wave good-bye to Mr Satan'.

Towards the end, the film grows more desperate. The pastors pray for a little girl who has always been paralysed from the waist down. Nothing happens. The pastors are clearly disturbed. They tell the parents to keep on having faith. Another woman brings her epileptic son. As the pastor prays, the woman begins to shake and speaks in an unknown tongue. 'What about me?' asks the son.

The events in the film are in themselves dramatic — but it was the presence of Pastor Weeks in the lecture room which made the viewing of the film an event in itself.

A year earlier I'd been trying to invent ways of persuading students to discuss films. Now, because of the context that had been created, there was no questioning of the need to discuss. The students were eager to hear what Pastor Weeks had to say — while Pastor Weeks, in talking primarily about his beliefs, produced some penetrating film analysis.

The first point he had to make concerned the apparent objectivity of the film. Mitchell's style of programme-making is as 'objective' as any in the media. He appears to be concerned simply to record the truth of what he sees and hears, to allow the material to speak for itself. Weeks accepted Mitchell's lack of bias but commented on the *selection* of the material. 'You see, these meetings in the film are meetings where seeking for divine healing is the sole objective. In other words, you have a congregation of more or less spectators, and you have those who are coming quite sincerely' (again Weeks includes the adverb because he feels he's dealing with a way-out idea) 'in the hope that their condition will be relieved by their coming to the front. But, of course, other people incorporate this in a more normal form of service. And other people do things in a more — I don't use the word critically — dignified way. They don't have people falling around all over the place.'

Pastor Weeks was touching indirectly on one of the

central problems of documentary film-making. He was
saying that no matter how apparently neutral the style
might be, the very choice of the material itself revealed a
bias. In this case the bias was towards the visually dramatic.
By isolating the more obviously dramatic qualities of a
pentecostal meeting, the film had torn particular events
out of a wider context — so that even though these dramatic happenings had been recorded undramatically, the
picture had been distorted.

Having talked about the problem of selection, Pastor
Weeks went on to discuss the way in which the presence
of a camera itself changed the events being recorded. 'You
see, in that kind of service, unless the camera is virtually
hidden, there's always either a sort of embarrassment, or
a sense of playing to the gallery. In this case, I think, if
anything, they've played it down. You see, in that sort of
meeting, and in the pentecostal fellowship in general,
people are allowed, not only allowed to, but they're
encouraged to express themselves. If the cameras had not
been there, they might have shouted a bit more.' He added,
'I think that to make an honest film, you'd have to arrange
it so that nobody knew they were being filmed. And you'd
have to come over a period, to make a film of the whole
life of a church. You couldn't come to one service and say
— we'll take this one, it's representative. In the same way
that you couldn't come to this college, and shoot a couple
of lectures, and say, this is what Bradford Art College is
doing twelve months of the year.'

One of Pastor Week's sharpest criticism of the programme concerned the experience of viewing. 'I always
think that in viewing a thing like this, when you see it on
a film, there's an awful feeling of detachment. Whereas if
you're in the actual service, you can sense the atmosphere
and the effect of it much better. We look at it here, very
coolly, very dispassionately, and we're not a part of it.'

The remark underlined the central confrontation of the
whole project. For here were we, consciously taking up a
cool, detached position, following Brecht's advice to
'closely observe the behaviour of these people'. But for the
pentecostals themselves, belief was reality. They were

saved and going to heaven: we weren't. It was their job to
save us. Whenever we met them, we were trying to look
at, define, delineate the nature of their reality: they were
trying to draw us inside it, to make us 'a part of it'.

After that first session, Pastor Weeks went back up to
his church to pray that God would use him to bring us to
an understanding of salvation. We analysed the notes one
of the students had made. What was, somebody asked, 'the
Scriptural way to receive the Baptism of the Holy Spirit?'
It was one of the questions we decided to ask him when
next we met.

4

During the project, Pastor Weeks became a kind of norm,
against which we could measure the statements we were
to receive from other people. He was the 'expert': nothing
was more revealing than the comparison between the
official line he gave us, and the experiences we were to
record from less professional pentecostals.

For example, when we questioned him about 'the
Scriptural way to receive the Baptism of the Holy Spirit', he
spoke in very vague, general terms.

'I do sincerely believe,' he said — once again using his
stock-phrase — 'that speaking in tongues is the sign that
someone has received what the Bible calls the Baptism of
the Holy Spirit. What it is — it's — let me put it as clearly
as I understand it, because I've had the experience myself
— it's not a trance condition where you lose sense of time
and the presence of other people and that sort of thing,
and as if the mind goes blank and it's taken over by some
other force.' (Later, he was to be faced by the experience
of a woman who did report a 'trance condition', and who
felt she had been 'taken over'.) 'It's rather — in my experience, and what I've heard many others say — that one
becomes conscious of being filled by the power of God,
and the English language, or indeed, one's mother tongue,
is inadequate to express what you feel. And then comes
this experience of speaking in another language, which
one doesn't know as the result of birth, intelligence or

education. And there's a great, an overpowering sense of conversation with God.'

Pastor Weeks knows that he's talking about one of the central experiences of the pentecostal faith. Indeed, it's the belief in speaking in tongues which distinguishes the pentecostals from other evangelical sects. If he's explaining pentecostal beliefs to aliens, then he's got to deal with the experience. But he's also aware that it's this belief that has led to the rejection of pentecostalism by other evangelical sects: and didn't the Apostle Paul himself, in the book of Corinthians, warn against practising the speaking of tongues in front of unbelievers, in case people said they were mad? And so his own language is hedged with qualifications, and the experience itself is summed up in the mundane phrase, 'conversation with God'.

A seventeen-year old girl, who wrote to one of the students in the group, describing her own experience, had no such inhibitions.

'On Sunday, Bob called anyone who wanted something from God out to the front, and as I knelt there at the front, pins and needles filled my feet and hands. There could have been a reason for my feet because I was sat on them, but not for my hands. I really believed God would baptize me, and he did, because a new joy and peace came into my heart and I started to speak in another tongue. You can't understand what you're saying, the words just flow from your mouth. . . It is Alan's twenty-first birthday tomorrow. I have got him some wing mirrors for his car. . .'

What's interesting about this description, in comparison with Pastor Weeks's, is the physical detail — the remark about the pins and needles in the hands and feet — and the entirely unselfconscious juxtaposition of the spiritual experience with the everyday events of ordinary life — the reference to the perfectly ordinary birthday present. We were to meet this juxtaposition again and again. Flat Yorkshire voices would describe events that might have occurred in the Holy Land in the first century. 'Eh, Elsie,' said a very old, matter-of-fact woman on one of the tapes, 'weren't it that man that kept t'dog-meat shop as were raised from the dead?'

Again, Pastor Weeks described his salvation.

'My mother came into contact with the apostolic church when I was about six. I was about seven when I made my first conscious alignment with this church, when I said, I'm going to follow this faith. But, of course, that early decision was, as I grew older, put to the test of investigation, as to what I'd been taught, whether it was true. In my early teens, in the Forces, I had to go on and ask myself, well, is it really true? Was it a real experience? Having gone through those years of testing and re-examination and re-thinking, I could only say that the decision I had taken when I was seven was something I was glad I had taken, and that all I'd gone into in the years subsequently had only confirmed me in that decision.'

The laboured phraseology is that of a man who's trying to make a personal experience sound as objectively respectable as possible. Phrases like, 'my first conscious alignment with this church' and 'those years of testing and re-examination and re-thinking' muffle the direct, personal statement. Pastor Weeks is saying, 'I'm really as intellectual as you are, and this is the conclusion I've reached.'

A first-year student, who turned out to be a practising pentecostal, was much more direct in his account of a similar experience. 'When I was quite young in Scotland, I was late for church, and one of these lads that were with us came in and said, have you been converted? I'd never thought about it before. And he said, well, do you believe in Jesus, and so on? Do you believe he came to save your sins, and so on? I said, yeh. He said, OK, then we'll pray. And he asked for forgiveness for my sins, and I asked Jesus to come into my life. It was all rather childish and so on, but now I've come to realise exactly what it means. I was about ten then, I think. The older I get the more meaning it has for me.'

Once again, it was the old woman who'd known the dog-meat man who was raised from the dead, who provided the most down-to-earth statement: 'I was saved in 1933, 2 July. I know I was saved because I was there when it happened.'

By far the most spectacular recordings we made were
concerned with miracles of healing. There was a woman, in
Bradford, who claimed to have been healed of a broken
leg — 'I saw this lump that was sticking out disappear' —
and also of multiple sclerosis. She told a long story, too -
afterwards one of the students said she'd got 'the gift of
the gab' — about how her daughter, Gale, had been unable,
as a child, to digest her food, how she'd gone blind through
a Vitamin A deficiency, and how they'd given the child
up as dying. But her husband had prayed, and the child
had suddenly begun to take her feeds — 'Her whole trouble
of digestion was instantaneously changed, and within a
matter of weeks, the child was beginning to look like a
normal baby.' What made the recording session a dramatic
event was the presence, in the living room, of Gale herself.
And Gale was still blind. The woman said she'd submitted
to the sovereign will in this matter, but that she still
believed God could give her faith 'for the healing of her
eyes'.

Pastor Weeks, as usual, had a very precise idea of what
healing was all about. 'Faith healing,' he explained, 'is
usually a term that covers people whose theology I
wouldn't say is mainstream Christian theology. In other
words, there are many people whose persuasions are spiritualist in their outlook who speak about faith healing, and
there are some who claim to have no religious beliefs at all
who talk about faith healing. The emphasis in such
attempts to help humanity is always on the individual
and the exercise of their faith — the power of mind over
matter. Whereas our emphasis is that we believe God can
heal. The fact that we exercise faith to seek for healing is
secondary.'

A girl who had been prayed over by Pastor Weeks had
little understanding of such subtleties. She said: 'What
they do is, you go out and you either sit at the front or
you kneel at the front, and they come and they pray and
they pour oil over you. It's supposed to heal you, the oil.
And they put their hand on you and they do something.
I don't know what it is. And they say something, and it's
supposed to heal you, or something.'

'How many times have you been to the front?' she was
asked. 'About four.' 'You were nervous the first time,
weren't you?' 'I was nervous on Sunday as well.' 'And do
you think it's done you good?' 'Yeh.' 'And how do you
feel, inside, you know?' 'Felt a bit funny.' 'Anything else
but funny?' 'Mm — not really. It started doing me good
after the first time I went to the front. I've been going to
foot exercises, but when I went the week before Christmas,
he said, I think you're walking better.'

The gap between Pastor Weeks's concept of divine healing, and the girl's concrete experience is as great as the gap
between what teachers imagine they're communicating to
pupils, and what the pupils actually learn.

But towards the end of the project we were to encounter
a still more dramatic confrontation — between Pastor
Weeks and a tape-recording we'd made of a woman who
wasn't a pentecostal at all.

The woman claimed to be a spiritual healer. She lived
in a small, terraced house, and was the mother of a girl in
fourth-year graphics. We came into contact with her
through a lecturer in college, a sculptor, who claimed that
she had brought relief to his back. She was a very quiet,
gentle woman, very reluctant to talk at first — she didn't
have 'the gift of the gab'. But when she did put her experiences on tape, they were at least as convincing as those of
the pentecostals.

She made her own position clear from the start. 'Spirit-
ualism,' she said, 'is a religion. I'm not a spiritualist. It
doesn't interest me, the religious part of it. It's the healing
that I'm mostly interested in. Some people have it as a
religion, but no. Not me.'

She had been cured, she said, of 'ulcerative colitis.' A
healer had visited her. 'All he did was lay his hands on me
— like that. That's all. And then he prayed and I relaxed.
But with spiritual healings, there are three of you and you
must blend — the patient, the spirit and the medium. It
was a gradual healing. It took about eight weeks to clear
up. He gave up his lunch hour to come and give me a healing every day. You felt this warm glow, and you'd just
think there was a ball of fire inside you.'

She had been told by three mediums that she 'had the gift'. 'I didn't believe them at first, but I thought, well, I'll try it and see what I can do. There's a man comes round every Thursday afternoon, and he couldn't speak a word when he first came. He wouldn't do anything. He just used to sit, solid, day after day. Yesterday afternoon, I went round the room saying all the words I could, and he was saying them after me. I got him to do a jig-saw puzzle, trying to make rugs — anything that would occupy his mind and overcome his speech impediment. . .' There were people, she said, she'd helped with blood-pressure, with rheumatoid arthritis, and with heart disease. And she'd done absent healings. 'There's a Madame Ivetty in France. I got what was wrong with her just by holding a letter. I can only ask for the complaints to be seen to. I don't know the results yet.'

We analysed the recordings we made of this woman, and compared them with the beliefs of Pastor Weeks. Although, like Pastor Weeks, the woman believed in miraculous healings, she lived in a completely different world of experience. Pastor Weeks talked about the power of God: she talked about a spirit who had once been a doctor in Manchester. Pastor Weeks had a coherent theology: she believed vaguely that you were put on this earth to do good and help people. And when the students asked her if she had ever been saved, she looked at them in bewilderment.

Yet the physical happenings she described were very like those of the pentecostals. We played the tapes to Pastor Weeks, and put this point to him.

He said, 'Well, of course, it does bring the thought to mind that there's not only God's power at work, but I believe that there's also a Satanic power; and going into the realm of the spiritual or the ethereal or the supernatural, or whatever you like to call it, trying to get into these realms can, I think, be dangerous if we're not approaching it in the proper Christian manner. In other words — what I believe in — let me put it quite frankly, you you may challenge me if you wish — but I believe the devil has power — Satan, Beelzebub, whatever you like to put to him or the evil force behind the world — but I do believe that this evil person the Bible calls Satan, that he too can exercise power to a degree, the end in view all the time being that he might prevent people from coming to what most Christians believe to be the truth about Christ and eternity.'

Pastor Weeks's discomfort is apparent in every hesitation and qualification. He *knows*, with absolute certainty, that supernatural things happen — and that they come either from God or the devil. And he also knows, since this woman doesn't approach the spiritual world in 'the proper Christian manner', that if there's any truth at all in her story, *she must be possessed by the devil.* But this is the Pastor Weeks who, throughout the project, has been posing as the rational, intelligent, common-sense person. Listening to her gentle, good-natured voice on the tape, he realises that to say, 'she's demon-possessed' will hardly cut much ice with these students he's been talking so sensibly with for a fortnight. And so he qualifies: 'ethereal, or whatever you like to call it', 'let me put it quite frankly, you may challenge me if you wish', 'whatever name you like to put to. . . the evil force behind the world.' And, instead of saying what he believes, that if you don't accept Christ you'll go to hell, he referes to 'what most Christians believe to be the truth about Christ and eternity.'

When Pastor Weeks had gone, for the last time, we examined particularly the way he used language to preserve the illusion that his own, highly idiosyncratic view of the universe was one that all reasonable people must share.

And some of the students began to pay attention to other idiosyncratic views as well.

5

For example, one student discovered a man who peddled Social Credit tracts around a transport cafe every morning. The student brought back some of these tracts, and the group began to examine them for ideas of salvation. Another took his tape recorder to Leeds United football ground and recorded an interview with a man who had once supported Sunderland. The man remembered the afternoon when he'd been changed into a Leeds United supporter. 'John Charles was my god', he said.

The danger was that the group would move into a position, not of watchful scepticism, but of cynicism about the validity of any beliefs or commitments. The lecture given by Dr Vyvyan Wyatt, the biologist from the university, put what we had been discussing back into perspective.

Dr Wyatt brought to his own discipline the same scrutiny that we had applied to the gospel material. 'I too am a believer', he said. He demonstrated the absurdity of the opening chapter of Genesis — but then went on to demonstrate the absurdity of what Charles Darwin had put in its place. Scientists believed that they could use the order of fossils in rocks to make a timetable of evolution: but if the fossils in a particular slab of rock appeared in the wrong order, they didn't abandon their beliefs. They explained that it was because of a fault.

At the end of his lecture, Dr Wyatt said that his excuse for believing in science was that it *worked.* He believed that if he turned a switch, the electric light would come on. As long as the electric light continued to come on when scientists said it would, he would continue to believe in the validity of the scientific method.

Dr Wyatt had demonstrated in his lecture that it was possible to commit yourself to a position while still maintaining a cool, sceptical awareness. But what also prevented the project from lapsing into a patronising cynicism was, first, the down-to-earth ordinariness of the believers who described these extraordinary events — they were the kind of people you might have played darts with in a pub, except for the fact that they went to the mission instead; and, secondly, the sheer sense of enjoyment in many of the pentecostal services.

The most entertaining event of the whole project was a visit to a Glory meeting. The Glory People have their headquarters in Newark, but they tour the country, holding meetings. They had hired a coach, and a hall in Bradford. They drove up from Newark singing and shouting; spent six hours in the hall, singing and shouting; then drove back again to Newark, in the early hours of the morning, still singing and shouting.

They had an accordion, a piano, an electric organ,
electric guitars and drums. The audience had tambourines.
The service consisted entirely of singing and shouting.
They sang the choruses, over and over again, hypnotically.
'He lives,' they sang,

> He lives, He lives,
> Jesus is alive in me;
> It is no longer I that liveth,
> But Christ that liveth in me.

At times, they left their seats and shuffled in a line
round the room, banging their tambourines and singing,
in what they called a 'Jericho march'. Some of them rolled
about the floor, laughing and speaking in tongues. Nobody
paid them any attention.

The Glory People didn't preach, and they didn't try to
convert anybody. They were too busy having a good time.
They were the pentecostal equivalent of doing your own
thing.

It was the joy of the Glory People that we were to take
as a starting point some years later, when we made our own
Hot Gospel show, *Looking Forward to 1942*. Like them,
we took the choruses and used them as a means of theatrical expression. At Wroclaw, student groups from Poland
and Yugoslavia and Holland were caught up by the pentecostal songs. Throughout an international theatre festival,
they could be heard singing.

> Lord, send the old time power,
> The pentecostal power,
> That sinners be converted,
> And Thy Name glorified.

7

The *Hot Gospel* project was one of the most successful
projects of that first year. It was successful because it confronted us directly with an experience that was complex,
contradictory, but very rich. It forced on all of us who

took part the fact that there were other ways of looking at the world from the one we normally accepted: and, in fact, it led us to question, from experience, the use of the word 'normal' at all. It was this exploration of a different way of life that gave the project its most obvious educational value.

But there was a third project that year which was to have a lasting effect on those involved. This was Adrian Mitchell's *Making Poetry Public*. It was a very personal project, and it grew directly from the students' response to Adrian, both as a poet and as a person. It was stamped with his own openness to experience.

The project was built around the idea that poems are presents you offer to friends. The final product consisted of a collective offering.

The group began by going for a walk. They spent a whole day making a circular tour of the hills that circle Bradford. They took notebooks and cameras. They wrote down words and phrases they encountered during the day, and they photographed words — street names, pub signs, phrases from newspapers, snatches of conversation. They spent an extended lunch-hour in a country pub putting together what they'd collected, then went on and collected more.

Back in college, they began to shape what they had noted down into a collective poem. They called it *Walkabout*. Each section dealt with a particular part of the walk. At the same time, Adrian Mitchell asked each of them to write an individual poem or song. It was to be completely personal, as a contrast to the collective work, and Adrian himself refused to make any judgements on anything the students wrote.

The students also made and collected objects, with the intention of filling the room with words. One made a rubbing of an epitaph on a local gravestone; another transcribed 'Eleanor Rigby' as if it were a Victorian wall text; yet another wrote words on an old boot. They also prepared gifts for the final event — Adrian Mitchell gave an old piano, which he had brought to the studio.

For the performance, they invited only friends. There was no playing space or audience space: the group would perform one episode of the poem, then move to another part of the room and perform the next. At each stop, the individual students read their own poems or sang their own songs. At the end, each member of the audience was offered a personal gift and a glass of wine.

The quality of the poems varied: but there was no doubt about the quality of the experience. Adrian Mitchell refers to it obliquely in a poem called *Leaflets*, which he dedicates to 'Brian Patten and my twelve students in Bradford'. It describes how, 'outside the plasma supermarket' he gives each of the shoppers a leaf. The shoppers react in different ways: 'The third says she is not interested in leaves. . . The fourth says, "Is it art?" '. The poem ends:

> But you took your leaf like a kiss.
> They tell me that, on Saturdays,
> You can be seen in your own city centre
> Giving away forests, orchards, jungles.

The poem captures precisely the mood of the project. After Adrian Mitchell had gone, the students formed themselves into a permanent group. They wrote poems, hired rooms in pubs, gave readings. Most of them had written poetry before: but the project had given them the courage to take themselves seriously. Later, one of the girls on the project, Angela Shepherd, was to write:

> It's stupid when you have to go to school
> And try to show them something and they think
>   you're just a fool.
> Because all they want to see is what they've seen before;
> And all you have to do
> Is just a little more
> Than what you ever do.
> Yes, it's a drag. . .

Most of the students on Adrian Mitchell's project — or, for that matter, on any of the projects — had been to schools where all they wanted to see was what they'd seen

before. They had emerged from the system, having learnt
nothing except that the system was not for them. One of
the most talented, Keith Knowles, had failed O-level
English more than once. Within two years Keith Knowles
had casually picked up O-level English, in case he might
need it sometimes, and was forcing me to discuss with him
a group of French poets, Baudelaire, Lautréamont,
Rimbaud, whom I hadn't read since I left Oxford. His
poems are full of energy, gaiety, and a farcical surrealist
logic. Above all, they have a personal directness that
reflects the way he speaks, his particular tone of voice.

Typical is a poem he wrote in his third year, *Leaving in
Ambulance No. 10:*

I'm a father,
I'm a father.
Yesterday my wife gave birth to a toy train set.
It weighed 12lb 9oz
And it went choo, chi, choo, che.
It's got the cutest little funnel
And it's the image of its mother;
When we take it out in the pram
Everybody says, what a bonny little train-set.
We've built him his own little station and a super-pink
    platform.
But he has his faults, like he keeps
Getting us up in the middle of the night
To re-stoke his little boiler;
And it's always me that has to
Chunt him and chunt him to sleep.
We're all so proud of him and his big beautiful blue
    carriages.
He chunts that he wants to be a
Car smasher on rail crossings when he grows up. . .
But doesn't every little train.
I can't help wondering though what sort of track he's
    going to run
And what sort of world he's going to puff in
With all these queer trains around.
Things are changing so quickly.

Things had certainly changed very quickly at Bradford during that first year of project work. From sitting in front of apathetic students, struggling to find new ways of engaging their attention, and of justifying my own existence, I'd stumbled into a world where people were suddenly discovering new sources of energy in themselves, and new ways of directing that energy. It seemed to me, in the summer of 1967, that we were on the edge of an educational breakthrough that would lead to radical changes.

At the end of the summer term we staged a mammoth 4 July event in Bradford. It began at ten o'clock in the morning and went on until four o'clock the following morning. There was a procession with a tatty American flag; a discotheque with Adrian Mitchell, called 'Swinging with Vera Lynn', poems by Adrian Henri, an abortive production of a play by John Arden, the Scaffold, exhibition boxing, a weight-lifter, a happening by Robin Page, a West Indian steel band, Ten Years After, Champion Jack Dupree. . . It all went on, unabated, over a period of eighteen hours.

It marked the culmination of a year's work in which we had begun to confirm Brecht's affirmation that 'all that can be said is that the contrast between learning and amusing oneself is not laid down by divine rule. It is not one that always was and must continue to be. There is such a thing as pleasurable learning, cheerful and militant learning.'

'Cheerful and militant learning' was an accurate description of the process all of us had been involved with in that first year's work.

Chapter three
A succession of events

'Neo-realist reality is incomplete, formal and above all, reasonable but the poetry, the mystery, all that completes and enlarges tangible reality is missing. "The most remarkable thing about fantasy", said André Breton, "is that it doesn't exist." '

Luis Buñuel, *Poetry and Cinema*

'When I got home from the second world war . . . I thought it would be easy to write about the destruction of Dresden, since all I would have to do would be to report what I had seen . . . but not many words about Dresden came from my mind then . . . I think of how useless, the Dresden part of my memory has become and yet how tempting Dresden has been to write about.'

Kurt Vonnegut, *Slaughterhouse Five*

1

At eleven o'clock in the morning on 2 November 1967, a dozen students suddenly appeared on the steps of the Queen Victoria monument in the centre of Bradford. They were all dressed in black — black jeans, black sweaters, black polythene capes tied round their necks, and they all wore red armbands. They climbed up the steps, turned round, and began to read aloud in unison from the thoughts of Chairman Mao. A policeman at the foot of the steps tried to pretend that nothing was happening.

At roughly the same time, two miles or so from the city centre, a procession of more than a hundred students, led by a chance band, came swinging through the gates of the park in which the city's main art gallery, the Cartwright

Memorial Hall, is set. These students, too, were dressed in black, but with white armbands. The girls had boots and long skirts that swung round their ankles, and they carried wooden home-made rifles. Behind them, in the procession, were four huge, twelve-foot puppets, made out of cardboard boxes painted black. The students carried slogans on banners: 'Support Your Government', 'Down with Red Agitators', 'No Peace With Aggressors'.

In the city bus station, a bus arrived from Barnsley. About twenty-five students, in black with white armbands, got off the bus and looked round. A van drove up, crudely camouflaged. Out of it leapt a student with a red armband. He picked out the four prettiest girls, told them to get in the van, and drove away. Inside the van, the girls had their white armbands exchanged for red.

Outside a bread shop in the city centre, a queue of two dozen students formed. They wore red armbands and carried the slogan 'Peace, Land, Bread'. Each student bought one teacake. Then they took their teacakes across the town to a disused post office that had been left to crumble in the middle of blocks of high-rise council flats. In the shop window were placards telling people they could take anything they liked from the shop, for free, and could leave anything they liked except money. A wordless poster showed Lenin reaching out over the Italianate city hall and the mills of Bradford.

The Russian Revolution in the streets of Bradford was the first event which called people's attention to the fact that something unusual in education was happening in the Art College. I'd never expected it to reach such proportions. I had, it's true, described it as an experiment in public drama: but I'd thought that about thirty students would be taking part. In fact, we had over three hundred, many of them from other art colleges in Yorkshire. I'd been round to a number of colleges describing the idea. All I asked students to do was to come dressed in black and to be willing to keep to the rules: but, in fact, many of them made elaborate black costumes. A large group from Leeds, including the two pop artists, Robin Page and Patrick Hughes, formed the core of the morning procession through the streets. They created a very sharp visual image: the day began in black and white.

The idea was that we would turn Bradford for a day into St Petersburg, and try to re-create, in the form of a dramatic game, some of the events of the October Revolution. The emphasis was on the word 'game'. We weren't, I knew, in any position to stage one of those huge Meyerhold street plays. Instead, I drew the analogy with children playing in the streets. When they play, say, cowboys and Indians around street corners, they're totally absorbed in their game. They fire bullets at each other and to them the bullets are real. Passers-by can walk through the game without interrupting it, without even noticing it. On the other hand, if they so wish, they can stop and watch. But the children don't explain the game, or perform it for the passers-by. In the same way, I didn't believe that we should explain our game. The play itself was the thing. The more seriously we played, I believed, the more impact we would have: but the game, and not the impact, was the central concern. If people wanted to stop and watch, so much the better: if they wanted to walk through the game and ignore it, that was their privilege.

A group of twenty-eight students began working seriously together only ten days before the event. We started with background. We looked at the *Potemkin* film, had lectures from university experts on Soviet history, listened to and argued with a militant Trotskyist. We also had in college Ron Hunt's exhibition on post-revolutionary art in Russia — *Descent into the Streets*. Ron Hunt himself gave us a lecture on the subject.

But the momentum of the project soon began to carry us away. I wanted to discuss, in some detail, not only the events of the revolution, but Meyerhold, Brecht and American street happenings. In fact, as it became clear we would be dealing with large numbers of students, the practical problems of organising the day began to preoccupy us entirely.

We divided into groups. One group worked at inventing the game. Another group, working with John Fox — who later formed England's first fine art theatre group, The

1. 'the day began in black and white. . .' ▶

Welfare State — built giant puppets. This was the first
event that John Fox had been involved in at Bradford —
I'd brought him over officially to act as tutor/librarian.
Without his energy, the event would never have taken
place.

A third group created a chance band, and a fourth
looked for, set up and managed the free shop. A young
lecturer, John Gascoigne, made himself responsible for
this: he was later to run a number of community events,
particularly in Bradford working-men's clubs.

For me, personally, the most interesting work was done
with a group of advertising students who were preparing
the poster. They hit on the image — Lenin over Bradford
— very quickly. All the discussion was about what should
go with the image. They wanted to have explanatory
titles: 'Coming soon — the Revolution in Bradford',
'November 2: Russian Revolution in the Streets'. I argued
that we weren't selling after-shave, and we weren't selling
a show. The poster should be an integral part of the event
itself. If the event was simply going to happen, then the
picture of Lenin should simply happen. Eventually, we
agreed to have no words at all, to allow the image to speak
for itself. In creating the poster, we looked at posters and
sweet wrapping by Mayakovsky. To me, working with
this group meant 'complementary studies' in the fullest
sense. The students were using their own skills, working
in their own medium — but the medium had been placed
in a different context in such a way that they were coming
at their own assumptions from a different angle. It was a
very Brechtian exercise.

The game itself turned out to be difficult to plan. The
problem was to keep the tension of a game, while preser-
ving the shape of a drama. We wanted the day to start
white and turn red.

Eventually, we divided the participants into two teams,
and gave them four locations to capture. A location would
be captured by whichever team had more bodies there —
one man can vote — on the stroke of the hour, but extra
votes, in the shape of red or white discs, could be won by
carrying out instructions that were handed out in envelopes.

Some of the instructions were practical: 'Find a real com-
munist and take him to the free shop'; some left room for
flights of the imagination: 'Take six bourgeois heads to
an agent in the technical college canteen'; 'Unite the
workers of the world'; 'Convert a goldfish'; 'Put down red
plots'. My favourite instruction was, 'Interview a journalist
and ask him what he thinks he is doing and why'.

In order to make sure that the red discs won, we printed
a lot more red discs than white. At the end of the day, the
steps of the Cartwright Hall, which had been turned for
the day into the Winter Palace, were covered in showers of
red discs. Lying bedraggled in the rain were the broken
heads of the white puppets. And, soaked to the skin, the
students who had formed the white procession in the
morning now formed a red procession, which marched
with banners, through Lumb Lane and the Pakistani
ghetto, to a final rally in a disused engine shed.

So far as making a public impact was concerned, the
day was an undoubted success. And it was successful in
that it involved large numbers of students in a theatre
event.

Judged as street theatre, it was, to my mind, patchy.
The events were too scattered around the city. We'd
wanted this — but the general sense people had of what
was going on depended very much on the bit they happened to see. If all they saw was a group of students building a cardboard tower — which was what the television
cameras, who, along with me, were fooled into going to a
wrong location, happened to see — then it was possible to
dismiss the affair as a student rag. But if what they saw
was a group of students walking seriously along a street,
carrying a huge, impressively-made puppet, then the effect
was totally different.

Perhaps what made the biggest effect in the end was the
free shop, because it was in a particular neighbourhood
and was kept going for several days. At first, people stood
around cautiously, not knowing whether or not to go in.
Then they began, not only taking, but bringing things. At
one stage, twelve yards of Harris Tweed appeared — when
the news reached college, lecturers were rushing to get

there first. Money which was on offer remained untouched until some schoolchildren came in and helped themselves. As we were closing, a woman said, 'You made us feel uncomfortable, refusing to take our money'.

At the end of the day, a student theatre group, from the Sorbonne, whom I'd met at the Zagreb Festival, performed their version of Gargantua, which had won the major award at Zagreb. The Library Theatre was packed with students still bubbling from the events of the day. When the play ended, I heard a student say, 'I'd no idea theatre could be *enjoyable*. It was as good as going to a football match.'

Many people have asked me what attitude the police took to our activities. They had, of course, been informed, but they kept sending for me and asking for details. Since I had no details until about twenty-four hours before the event, I had to keep stalling. Finally, I went to the City Hall and told them what we were planning. When I'd finished, they said, 'Is that all?' Then they produced a fat file. They said, 'You're not going to put up barricades in Forster Square? Or drop flour bags from the top of the multi-storey car-park?' They had a list there of every wild suggestion that had ever been made while we were preparing the event.

It turned out that the son of a policeman was in one of the groups. It would, in fact, have been a good tactic to plant a lot of wild rumours, so that when the final plan had come out, the police would have seen it as very mild, and accepted it in relief. This is what, in the event, happened — except that it was by accident, and we couldn't claim to have been so clever.

The police were finally very involved in the event. When I talked about letting off fireworks from high buildings, an officer said, 'But would that be effective in daylight?' I said I didn't know. 'Why don't you got to the top of Smith Street and try it?' he suggested, with interest. 'But would that be legal?' I asked. 'No', he said. 'But I should try it anyway.'

The police solemnly accompanied all our processions. They became part of the theatre. When it was over, two of them said they hadn't enjoyed themselves so much for a long time.

Policemen, too, must get very bored on the streets of Bradford. And when they're bored they pick up students at random and search them for pot. Perhaps educationalists should provide more street games for the police — to keep them out of mischief.

2

The Russian Revolution was undoubtedly the biggest and most widely-publicised of our events in that second year: but it was only one among many. For if, in the first year's activities, it had mainly been a question of finding new ways of working, creating new structures, and exploring new possibilities, the eighteen months that began in September, 1967, was a period in which imagination that had previously been stifled was suddenly turned loose. Ideas seemed to pour out of people, both teachers and students. The place was peopled with visiting artists, who brought all kinds of clashing enthusiasms. One night, in the local pub, I counted Adrian Mitchell, who'd come to do a reading, Jeff Nuttall, the author of *Bomb Culture*, Michael Duane, the ex-headmaster of Risinghill, Cornelius Cardew, the avant-garde musician, Paul Walton, the author of a new Penguin on Marxism, Tony Earnshaw, co-author of a sur-realist book, *Musrum.* . . . It was no special occasion: they weren't all together. They just happened to be around at the same time, working on various courses in the college.

We produced a succession of events. We ran a Festival of Chance: each day a different visitor created a chance event. John Lathan brought an abstract film: we made a sound-track, banging tins, chairs, anything that made a noise, while the dark lecture theatre was lit up by the rhythmic blobs of light from the screen. Robin Page experi-mented with scenes in which somebody read an article from a newspaper, while somebody else performed actions at random. Sometimes the random actions and the words coincided to form funny and strange images. Cornelius Cardew made what he called music by moving all the objects from one half of a room into the other half, including the window frames and doors. He recorded the activity. Some of the events might well have qualified for *Private Eye's* pseuds' corner: but out of the free flow of the situation emerged projects that were hard-centred and fully worked out.

So: we invented a religion. Two religions, in fact, since the group broke up after the first day into rival sects. This was a follow-up of the *Hot Gospel* project: several of the same students took part. One religion — the Apostolate of Gui — grew from the idea, invented by a student, John Booth, of the self-imprisoning god. God was uranium. He had voluntarily imprisoned himself in nature, and had invented the whole process of evolution so that man could become intelligent enough to release the god. It seemed to me at least as sensible as the idea of a god who invented human beings so that he could have himself crucified.

The other religion was invented by Tony Earnshaw and a group of girls. They called themselves the Dreamers of Farmer-Reaper, and their creed was essentially passive, gentle, tolerant. The world, they said, was really a farm, owned by the Farmer-Reaper, who lived on our dreams. While we slept, he fed. He had constructed the world in such a way that somebody was always asleep. Our only purpose in waking life was to make good dreams for Farmer-Reaper — but since nobody knew what he thought to be good dreams, they felt there was very little they could do to help him. They agreed that they knew very little about him. They were happier for knowing about him, and felt other people would be happier, too. But they didn't want to convert anybody. They wanted to look at movies — 'movies are material dreams'. They collected Ovaltine and Horlicks packets.

The Dreamers invented a service. They put a paper bag over your head and a glass in your hand. The glass contained cold Horlicks, but you weren't to know this, since you were asked to drink it before you took the paper bag from your eyes.

You were led to a seat. A tape-recorder told dreams (they'd recorded a girl telling her own dreams earlier in the project). When you'd drunk the Horlicks and removed the paper bag, you saw *King Kong* being played backwards and silent on a cinema screen. Beneath the cinema screen were two television sets, playing whatever happened to be on at the moment, with the sound turned down.

Gradually sound was faded in: the sound of *King Kong* backwards, the sounds of the TV programmes, a Rolling Stones record. People were given tin cans, sticks, sheets of metal and encouraged to add to the noise. As the noise increased, the Dreamers shouted, danced, sang and ran up and down, trying to make themselves tired. Presently, the noise began to fade. The Dreamers lay down, one by one, on beds that they'd placed on the floor in the corners of the room. *King Kong* played on, backwards and silent.

It was a good religion to take part in. It was pleasant to lie there, at the end, sleepy, and open your eyes from time to time to see this huge gorilla carrying a girl backwards. . . But when the Dreamers invited non-believers at the end of the project, they found that if people sat there, silent and hostile, they themselves didn't possess the performance skills to make the event work.

Later, we invented an alien intelligence. This was, by definition, impossible: so we put bits of paper, with imagined qualities of intelligence written on them (e.g. all intelligences drink water every fifteen minutes) in a hat, drew out five bits of paper, and made the intelligence from that. For some reason, this project became entangled with a project for the British Film Institute at the National Film Theatre where we had been asked to spend a day demonstrating how we used film. So we spent a lot of time looking at films through the eyes of alien intelligences. *Twelve Angry Men* became a search for water. Tony Earnshaw had invented a huge, green lizard, which was keeping us all like hens, and fattening us up for food. His description of *High Noon* was that the creatures seemed to be well cared-for — they all wore fancy feathers — but that the farm itself seemed to be very badly kept: the creatures were always leaving their hen-huts and walking up and down the streets, brandishing things at each other. When a shot of the railway line, vanishing into the distance, appeared on the screen, Tony Earnshaw was heard to say, 'There you are. I told you the farm was badly kept. The fence has fallen down.'

We made a film ourselves involving scale. Chris Vine, who was later to become the funniest performer in the Theatre Group, made a huge ruler and a huge pencil. He then sat in front of a camera, investigating his hands and feet, and other parts of his body, while the huge pencil pushed in objects for his consideration — the boot from Adrian Mitchell's poetry project, a loose arm from a model, a brush. The pencil pointed to his activities. It was clearly being wielded by some giant observer. At the end of the film, the huge ruler was lowered behind him, indicating that he was only one and a half inches high.

Later, we used a huge transparent ruler to measure movies. We hung it down the middle of the screen. It indicated the height of the characters, measuring them both in long-shot and close-up. What was interesting was that, if the film was a bad one, you remained conscious of this ruler for a long time. If the film was good, you forgot about it. When, at the National Film Theatre, somebody asked how you measured students' progress, Patrick Hughes waved his hand at the ruler on the screen.

Another group became involved in the movie criticism. This was a group working on *1984*, with Michael Randle. Michael Randle had been the brains behind the Committee of 100, which led civil disobedience against the H-bomb in the sixties. He had spent, all told, several years in jail. I was delighted when he agreed to stop going to jail and to come and work in the complementary studies section. In between going to jail and editing *Peace News*, Michael Randle had acquired a university degree, and done work on linguistics. With the students he set about inventing Newspeak. They produced a series of posters with Big Brother's ten commandments: one, I remember, was, 'Number 6 — OXFAMISE RUBBISHWEAR'. They wrote a newspaper in Newspeak, and while we were working on the alien intelligence, they too turned their attention to the films. Their analysis of *High Noon* begins: 'BIG BROTHER IS. Newsoc primedays big brother exinpartmem

2. *Big Brother poster from Michael Randle's Newspeak project, 1968.* ▶

1 Big Brother is Love

goodkeeper show crimethink tends. Attend ownthinkmeet to co habitate prole unmale. Show crimethink sexfeel. No ungood thoughts show at proledocnate meet till ex-goodkeeper attend. . . Goodthinkers bellyfeel Big Brother Love.'

All of these events were so entertaining in themselves that it would have been easy to underestimate — as, I think, the NFT audience did — the amount of hard, intellectual work that went into their preparation. 'But what are they *learning*?' the Principal would ask me — a question repeated by some of the teachers at the NFT conference. Well, they — we — were learning how to dream up ideas; and, having dreamt them up, how to put them into operation. The process involved research, thinking, a use of the collective imagination, analysis, organisation, making objects, the acquiring of technical skills to make it all work. And the ideas themselves were involved with a re-examination of things in our society which we had always accepted as normal — and which now, looked at through the eyes of a Dreamer, or of an alien intelligence, or of a goodthinker from 1984, seemed very strange and unacceptable indeed. We were using happenings and events and educational projects in the way that Brecht had wanted to use theatre.

One event, at any rate, during that period, found general acceptance — with the educators, the administration, and a section of the local community. This was an event called *The Survivors*. It was directed by John Gascoigne, and eventually took the form of a celebration of the fiftieth anniversary of the end of the First World War on 11 November, 1918.

The original aim of *The Survivors* project was to collect as much material on tape as possible from people who had fought in the First World War, and who were still alive. Soon there would be none of them left: nobody would be living who had actually been there. The recordings would be historic documents in themselves, even if some of the stories were apocryphal. They would be evidence of how old people remembered dramatic and horrific events in which they were involved when they were young.

We put a letter in the local paper, and invited veterans

to contact us. There was no lack of replies. For days after, old men would wander into the college with medals and lumps of Mesapotamian sand. John Gascoigne and the students collected, during the fortnight's project, about forty hours' worth of tape.

After the fortnight was officially over, they began to prepare the event. Two or three of them edited the material down to a tape lasting one and a half hours. This involved a great deal of close and detailed work — listening to the tapes, deciding painfully what to leave out, putting the selections together in a way that made sense, going through the physically laborious work of putting the final programme together. Whenever after that English teachers asked me whether or not I forced people to write essays, and, if I didn't, how did I ensure disciplined work, I used to think of the hours this group spent together. Throughout my whole school and university career, I'd never worked with that kind of commitment — and these were supposedly non-academic students working at this as a sideline.

While the editing was going on, other members of the group were working in various ways. One was photographing a collection of slides that were to be synchronised with the final tape. Others were making posters to advertise the event, and having programmes printed. Still others were collecting costumes. The group booked a pub, hired films, contacted the survivors, and did all the organising entirely on their own initiative.

When the night arrived, the people who had contributed to the tape arrived with their wives and friends at a room over a pub. The room had been decked out with First World War posters. Girls wearing khaki jackets, and poppies, and mini-skirts, were there to serve drinks. The survivors listened to themselves on a tape which had been shaped to make a dramatic story. The tape was synchronised with the slides, and with a sequence from Pabst's *Westfront 1918*. Afterwards, they saw Charlie Chaplin's *Shoulder Arms*. A group of old ladies from a district of Bradford called Idle — they described themselves as *The Idle Ladies Concert Party* — sang 'By the light of the silvery moon' and told dirty jokes. The students sang songs from *Oh What A Lovely War.* The survivors offered songs of their own: 'There's a rose that grows in no-man's-land. . .'.

Very late that night, long after the pub had officially closed, old people and young students sang together round a concertina. In any other context, the old soldiers would have described the students as long-haired layabouts; while the students would have dismissed the old soldiers as boring old fogeys. The project and the event had brought them together to share in a common experience. It was one of our first genuine community theatre events.

2

The Survivors event took place in November 1968. It was a great success, though to me there was something lacking. The evening was nostalgic and anecdotal. It offered memories of the victims. But for a long time before that, a group of us had been working on a show that was intended to present the victims in relation to the political and historical forces that had victimised them. This show was called *A Carnival for St Valentine's Eve*, and dealt with the destruction of Dresden, on 13-14 February, 1945. We had first presented it on 13 February 1968, but had been very dissatisfied with the result. The show continued to obsess us for a long time.

The Dresden project was both a culmination of work that had gone on in our theatre workshops for nearly two years, and a taking-off point for a more disciplined approach to performance. After the first presentation, we realised that we had failed to communicate our ideas. During the next few years, developing own own kind of performance skills became a major preoccupation for the handful of students who were eventually to form the Bradford Art College Theatre Group.

The theatre workshop activities had begun where the *Performance* game left off. We moved from the slightly accidental quality of the game situation to the creation of sharp, theatre images. One which was particularly effective was an image of the Vietnam war as a circus. In putting it together, we used material from our own improvisations, together with two speeches originally written by Charles Wood for Peter Brook's *US* which Brook had never used. It involved a circus band of clowns, which turned into soldiers machine-gunned in battle; a President Johnson who popped out of a huge tea-chest, like a jack-in-the-box, and delivered one of the Charles Wood speeches: 'I'm in agony, agonisin', trying to decide whether to bomb or not to bomb. . . No, I have not lost my legs. No, I have not lost my head. . .'; a character called Charlie, who stood like a ring-master, uttering more Charles Wood: 'I think I'm Vietnam. . . Once knew a man thought he was France. Another thought he was Ghana. . . . Once he knew the lingo, he rattled away like a green beret. We call them berries. . .' A tight-rope walker picked his way between the two figures and amongst the dead bodies, while a drum beat, slowly. The scene must only have lasted about four minutes. It was the distillation of hours of improvisatory work — on war scenes, circus acts, the telling of fables. We'd put it together as a collage, taking single lines from several different improvisations, and juxtaposing them. This collage technique was one we were later to use in full-length shows, such as *Looking Forward to 1942* and *John Ford's Cuban Missile Crisis*.

Another workshop project that took us several steps forward was one, in which, for the first time, we used images from movies, at a pace that tried to create the sense of the fluidity of a film. We'd spent more than a week on work that seemed to be taking us nowhere: improvisations of scenes between masters and servants; between people in coffee bars; between policemen and middle-class house-wives. Finally, I got the idea of starting from where we were, which was nowhere. We'd be ourselves, sitting around in the studio, grasping for ideas, and one of the students, Doug Lawrence, would set up a number of scenes with himself as the hero. He'd say, 'Let's do the one where we climb a mountain, and a comrade slips and hurts him-self, and I carry him down to safety. . .' The only rule was that whatever situation Doug Lawrence set up would end in failure — failure for him, the hero.

At once, the work took off. Within a week, we'd put
together a show involving scenes from movies, always set
up by Doug Lawrence. He rescued a girl who'd been tied
to a railway track: the train ran over him. He was a famous
doctor, performing an operation on his sweetheart's
father: he sneezed at a critical juncture, and killed him.
He was the hero in a western gun-fight: the villain ducked
at the wrong moment and the hero was shot by his own
deputy. In a final scene, he led an escape from a prisoner-
of-war camp, through a tunnel, made of chairs. The
German rearranged the chairs so that they formed a perfect
circle. Doug found himself catching up the last member
of his own escape party. 'Somebody's caught me, Captain,'
shouted the escaper. 'Well, shoot him, you fool,' cried
Doug.

The group simply used whatever props were to hand in
the studio. What made the thing work was that they never
pretended to be anything except themselves playing at
being other people. It went right back to the basics of
theatre — one group of people playing at being another
group of people for the sake of a third group — the audience. And because the convention was so clearly established,
all the props could be pretend props — a piece of wood
could become a gun, an iron pipe could be a violin. Much
of the wit of the show came from this play with objects,
which later became a key element in the group's style.

There was, though, an added dimension to the show,
which came from the fact that the actors were always
clearly themselves as well as the characters they were playing. One of the girls, a beautiful Malayan, was black. As
the improvisations developed, she became the one who was
always responsible for Doug's downfall. She drove the
train which ran over him; in the last scene, she was the
guard who made the tunnel into a circle. As each scene
went wrong, Doug would stop it, explain to her that she'd
made a mistake, and then set up the next scene. This
relationship between Doug and the black girl became the
real centre of the show. At first, he would be very polite
and gentle: 'I know you can't help it, you've not had the
benefit of an English education, it's just the way you're

made.' But, as the girl kept winning more and more episodes, Doug would become increasingly unrestrained. By
the end of the performance, he was shouting, 'You stupid
wog! They should send you back where you came from. . .'
Eventually, we got to a last line in which Doug shouted
at her, 'Give me that bloody passport. I'll tear it up.' He
always failed, of course. In the last performance we ever
gave, Doug came to the last line and shouted, 'Give me
that bloody passport'. Fatima grinned and said, 'I've forgotten to bring it'. Doug shouted, 'You know you're supposed to give me the bloody passport so that I can fail to
tear it up. You stupid wog!'

What was interesting to me about the 'anti-hero' show
was the way it was working on two levels: on the level of a
series of funny scenes, performed at great speed — but also
on the level of the (carefully-rehearsed) relationships of
the people who were performing. This multi-dimensional
quality was one that we consciously aimed at in our later
work. It led to some interesting debates with professional
theatre-people about what was meant by 'acting'.

It was this theatre workshop group which finally put
together the Dresden show, together with a handful of
other students who hadn't, in the first place, been interested in the theatre work at all. The idea was that we'd run
a fortnight's research programme on the destruction of
Dresden, collect a lot of material, and then hand the
material over to the theatre workshop. What happened
in practice was that the theatre-workshop group involved
itself in the research, and most of the researchers went on
to involve themselves in the theatre.

Dresden was a particular obsession of my own. Years
later, a Dutch playwright was to give me a copy of Vonnegut's *Slaughterhouse Five:* on the fly-leaf he wrote, 'To
one who also will never get Dresden out of his mind'.

Slaughterhouse Five hadn't been written when I first
heard about Dresden, or when we first began to work on
the subject: but when I read it, the book defined for me a
whole lot of things we'd been trying to say in our show.

What had always obsessed me about Dresden was the
rational irrationality of the catastrophe — that and the fact

3. 4. *'The group used whatever props were to hand. . . . This play with objects later became a key element in the group's style.'*

that, on one February evening in my own life-time, a centuries-old city had been standing intact at quarter-past ten, and had been turned into the centre of a firestorm by ten-thirty. People in England didn't seem to be aware of what had happened. Everybody knew about the death camps, but in spite of David Irving's book, *The Destruction of Dresden*, from which I'd first learned the details of the raid, people I talked to about the event always said things like, 'Well, the Germans bombed Coventry' as if that were the end of the matter. And as if there were any real comparison between the Luftwaffe's activities over Britain — unpleasant and murderous though they were — and the systematic massacre of half a million German civilians carried out by the RAF from 1942 onwards.

The first idea I had was to stage a mock-Nuremberg trial of those responsible — particularly Churchill and Harris. (Harris himself had once imagined such a possibility: in his book, *Bomber Offensive*, he writes that no general welcomes the outbreak of a war. If he's victorious, he'll be pensioned off, if he loses he'll be hanged.) The charge, taken from Irving's book, would have been that Churchill had had Dresden put on the target-list because he wanted to frighten Stalin at the Yalta Conference, and that, once the machinery had been set in motion, Harris had carried out the raid, even though the weather hadn't cleared until after Yalta, because he wanted to destroy the few German cities that remained, and to kill as many Germans as possible.

The idea of a trial was appealing: David Irving himself was interested, and came to work with us on the project. But I abandoned it eventually, partly because it would have taken us into complex legalistics, which could have taken up most of the time available; partly because it would have involved an event built mainly round words, which I thought, we weren't at that stage equipped to deal with; and partly because I felt that the essential absurdity of Dresden couldn't be communicated through rational argument. It needed images: images as surrealistic as the events themselves.

Children in carnival clothes are found heaped up in

cellars, poisoned by carbon-monoxide; German fighter-pilots sit in their planes on brightly-lit runways waiting for orders to take off, while a huge bomber stream passes overhead — the orders never come, and no bombs are dropped on the runways, which aren't in the target area; horses from a circus are trapped in a ring of flame; in the air over the city, a cultured English voice says, 'Nice bombing, Plate-Rack force'; a man is hit on the head by the top of a railway carriage carried by a whirlwind down the street; a youth leader, in a train in the station, explains to refugee children the significance of the red target-marker bombs — and then realises that they're in the area that's been marked; vultures escape from the zoo and eat carcasses on the river; the main bridge across the river survives, and the railway, the ostensible target, is working again in forty-eight hours; they're still digging the bodies out in May. . .

How to communicate something of this? *And* the fact that Dresden was a culmination of a rational policy decided on by Trenchard in the 1920s. *And* enough of the history of bombing from Guernica onwards to put the story in perspective. *And* information about the political in-fighting that had surrounded the bomber offensive since Harris's appointment in February, 1942. *And* that this wasn't ancient history, that the B-52s over Vietnam were a logical extension. The material was all there for a major epic. All that was needed was a way of putting it all together. Which, of course, we never found.

3

We did, however, find considerable value, in the first place, from doing the research on the material. The research took two main directions. First, we worked through the written and photographic material that David Irving himself provided; and, secondly, we talked to and recorded the experiences of bomber crews.

The three days Irving spent with us were in every way remarkable. He was unhesitatingly generous with all his research material, and handed it all over to us in a huge pile. It was very instructive for the students to see what detailed research meant. Irving was the kind of researcher who would write a letter to someone asking where they were at ten-fifteen on the night of 13 February 1945, and, when he got a reply, would then write another letter saying 'When you say you were on such and such a street, do you mean you were on the left side walking east or the right side. . .'. Irving had pursued his subject for years with a commitment amounting to obsession. He had the target maps for all the major raids, showing the ostensible targets — factories, docks, railways — and the real targets — vast areas of working-class houses. And he had a wide collection of photographs, taken in Germany during and after the raids, most of which had never been published, and which he put at our disposal.

He was consumed with enthusiasm. When we watched *The Dambusters* with him for background information, he stopped the film at the climax of the raid, and pointed to a hut by the edge of the dam. 'I've interviewed the man. who was in that hut,' he said, and he told how Barnes-Wallis had complained that the film was inaccurate, and that they'd shown three bombs hitting the dam, for dramatic effect. One bomb, Irving said Barnes-Wallis had assured him, dropped accurately, would have been enough.

Later, two members of a bomber crew came in to make a tape-recording. 'Can you remember any particular raid you were involved in?' a student asked, as an opening question. 'Well,' came the reply, 'I remember the Peenemunde raid. . .'. 'Ah, the Peenemunde raid,' said Irving, who had written a book on the subject, and, picking up some chalk, he gave an hour-long lecture. The two ex-RAF men watched in wonder: nobody had ever shown any interest in what they'd done for more than twenty years. When Irving finally paused, one of them remarked, 'Well, all I remember is that there was a spoof raid on Berlin that night.' 'Here the memory plays one false,' said Irving, and added diagrams of all the spoof raids.

Irving's letters and documents and photographs gave us a very vivid picture of what had been happening on the ground, in the German cities, during the war. From the former bomber crews, we tried to build up a picture of what was happening in the air.

As with the *Hot Gospel* tapes, we were very careful not to take up any preconceived moral position. We concentrated on asking simple, concrete questions: 'How did you come to be in Bomber Command?' 'What kind of aeroplanes did you fly?' 'What was your job?' 'Can you describe exactly what you did?' 'What was it like to be in a plane over Germany at night?' 'Were you afraid?'

The picture that emerged was as vivid as the picture we'd got of the bombed cities. Most of the men we talked to had joined the RAF in 1940, because they were seized with the image of the fighter pilots, the 'few', who, in their Spitfires and Hurricanes, had protected the people of this island. All of them had wanted to fly fighters — but it was the growing bomber force that needed men. So they found themselves in large, often very cold heaps of metal over Germany, being shot at, avoiding searchlights, and often doing very mundane, boring jobs. A navigator described how he sat at a table with maps and a pencil. Over his head was a light. That was all he ever saw when he was on a mission. One night, a piece of flack had made a hole in the side of the plane above his table and just missed his head. He was afraid, he said, all the time: but the moment of worst panic he ever had was on the parade ground in Canada, when he was waiting to be given his wings. Alphabetically, his name was way down the list — and he was suddenly sure that he was going to be failed in front of everybody.

What was clear from all the interviews was that, on a mission the bomber made a little world of its own. The crews were, naturally, entirely preoccupied with doing the dangerous job they'd been given to do, and getting out as fast as possible. There was a total gap between their immediate, concrete experience, and the experience of the people on whom the bombs were dropping.

One afternoon during the project, this gap was, quite accidentally, closed. A former bomb-aimer had been describing his job for us. Afterwards, he wandered through from the recording room into the main studio. On the table in the studio, neatly laid out, were photographs of

corpses in the Hamburg streets, clutching at suitcases,
and of dead children, carefully placed in piles, in a gymna-
sium. The bomb-aimer picked up the photographs and
studied them. Then he said, 'My God, is that what we were
doing?'

4

By the time we'd gathered the material together, it was
clear that we wouldn't be able to create a full-scale show
in time to commemorate the event on St Valentine's Eve.
We were very committed to this commemoration, and so
we decided to settle for one image around which we would
build the event.

   The image was provided by Robin Page. Robin Page had
been a painter, sculptor, and cartoonist. But recently, he'd
created a number of theatre images, which he'd presented
in pubs, and during evenings of entertainment. One of
them involved a description of a battle. He'd recorded the
description on tape, slung the tape-recorder on his back,
with a wire to his ear, and had then spoken the words fed
to him by the tape-recorder, while he knocked over glasses
of water and produced images of destruction, at random.
We recorded an account of the raid, taken from Irving's
book, built a city out of cardboard boxes, and planned
for Robin Page to destroy the city while he told the story,
with the recording strapped to his back.

   The evening was a disaster, from which we learnt a great
deal about performance. We'd hired a theatre and an electrician, to work the lights. The electrician caught the flu,
and forgot to tell anybody, so that there was nobody who
really knew how to work the lighting. At one point, the
stage blacked out. The navigator — who'd been afraid he
wouldn't get his wings — had been asked to give a talk as
part of the show and spoke from a blacked-out stage. The
slides only arrived ten minutes before the show was due to
begin. The student who was handling them put them
through at random. Many of them were upside down.
Students in the audience turned their programmes into
paper aeroplanes, which they threw around the theatre —

at least they were entering into the spirit of the evening.

The only things that worked were the talk in the dark by the ex-navigator, which was impressive because of its openness, and Robin Page's individual demonstration of destructive art. People who saw the event said the ideas were great, but the execution lamentable. This was the origin of one of the Bradford legends: that we could think things up, but that we couldn't carry them out.

In spite of this traumatic experience, we went on living with the Dresden material for a long time after that. We kept the central image of the destruction of the cardboard-box city, but, when Robin Page dropped out after that first performance, we replaced him with a visible narrator, Keith Knowles (from the *Making Poetry Public* project), who sat at a table to one side of the action, reading Irving's account of the raid, while the boxes were destroyed.

We tried out a great many versions of the show. This became my favourite: in the centre of the stage was a screen, on which slides could be projected. To the left of the screen were two huge maps, one of Europe, showing the bomber routes, and one of Dresden, showing the target area — a sports stadium which pointed the way to the Inner City. The maps were kept covered until the show began. To the right of the screen was a high platform, with four chairs and a table, on which was set out a game of Monopoly.

An actor entered, dressed in RAF officer's uniform. He tore the covers from the maps, and briefed the audience on the raids. He treated the audience as if they were going to be the bomber crews. Then he climbed on to the high platform, and began to play Monopoly by himself. He kept on playing throughout the performance.

Five actors marched on in a line. The first had a RAF cap. The first one briefed the second in line, and then passed the hat on to the second, who briefed the third, passing the hat to the third — and so on. As the briefings went down the line, the original order was gradually softened. So, the first man simply said, 'Bomb Dresden: destroy the city', the second said, 'Bomb military installations in the city of Dresden. . .'. By the time the instructions had reached the last person in the line, they ran: 'In the city of Dresden there's a poison gas factory and a Gestapo HQ. Bomb them.' (We'd played this game in theatre workshops, using Herod's order to kill the male children of Bethlehem and Judea as a starting point. By the time the order reached the end of the line, it sounded as though the executioners were doing the children a favour. . .)

When these orders had been given, each of the five men stepped forward and described, in a brief statement, his job in the bomber. We took these statements direct from the recordings we'd made of the bomber crews.

The lights on stage went out, and a slide of Dresden was put on the screen — Dresden as it was before the raid. It was alternated with a slide of the ruined city. In front of these alternating slides, in the dark, was built a mysterious looking structure, of boxes. The structure was like one of those structures built with wooden bricks by children — in fact, I'd got the idea of the general shape by asking my own children to build me a city with their bricks. The structure destroyed the slide, and distorted it into strange shapes on many levels.

The structure was built by a girl who kept stopping in her building to make statements on behalf of the inhabitants of Dresden: 'There was a circus in Dresden. Horses from the circus were trapped in a ring of flame. . .', 'There was a firestorm in Dresden. . .'. When the structure was completed, she sat down amongst the mysterious shapes.

Suddenly, the lights came up, harsh. The slide image was destroyed, the mysterious shapes were revealed as Heinz baked-beans boxes. The officer playing Monopoly, stood up, and held a long peice of silver tinsel. 'You know what this is,' he said. 'It's called Window. We shovelled tons of it out over Germany to confuse the enemy radar. We'd known about it for years, but hadn't used it in case the Germans found out about it. Funny thing is, the Germans had known about it, too, and they hadn't used it in case we found out about it. . . On the night before the Hamburg raid, Churchill came to bomber HQ and said, "Open the window. . .".'. The actor threw the tinsel down over the structure. The girl picked it up and draped it over

her shoulders. As she did so, she said, 'There was a carnival
in Dresden on the night of the raid. Children dressed themselves in carnival clothes and wandered about the streets. . .'

The lights dimmed again. A bell rang. Keith Knowles
entered with a book, an alarm clock set at ten-fifteen,
which he set going, and a metronome. He began to read
Irving's account of the raid. Gradually, the five RAF men
came on to the stage. They came on one by one. Each
began, in his own way, to destroy cardboard boxes. So,
one sawed the corners from all the boxes; one flattened
them with an iron bar; one sat throughout the entire raid,
with a pair of small scissors, cutting one single box into
tiny strips. All of them concentrated entirely on the act of
destruction, which they carried out methodically. As the
destruction went on, the lights on the stage became continuously brighter and harsher. The girl with the tinsel
draped round her hair and shoulders sat perfectly still.

The destruction continued for eighteen minutes —
exactly the length of the first raid — and then the alarm
clock rang. Keith Knowles closed his book, picked up his
equipment and left. The destroyers also left the stage.
Throughout the destruction, the officer on his high platform had continued to play Monopoly, and two girls, in
brightly-coloured mini-skirts, had painted coloured aeroplanes, in the style of young children's drawings, all over
the two maps.

The girl with the tinsel was left alone amongst the ruins.
She stood up, very slowly, and then sang, 'Tomorrow is
St Valentine's Day. . .', Ophelia's song from *Hamlet*.
When she had left, the officer climbed down from his high
platform, took off his hat, and read out a very academic
letter that David Irving had written to *The Times*. The
letter was discussing whether or not the number of people
killed had been 100,000 or only 33,000. . .

We presented versions of the Dresden event similar to
this to a large number of audiences. What we found was
that the more people felt they knew about Dresden, the
less they responded to the actual images. So, when we
produced the event at the ICA, we were told by a group of
communists that we'd got it all wrong: that Dresden had

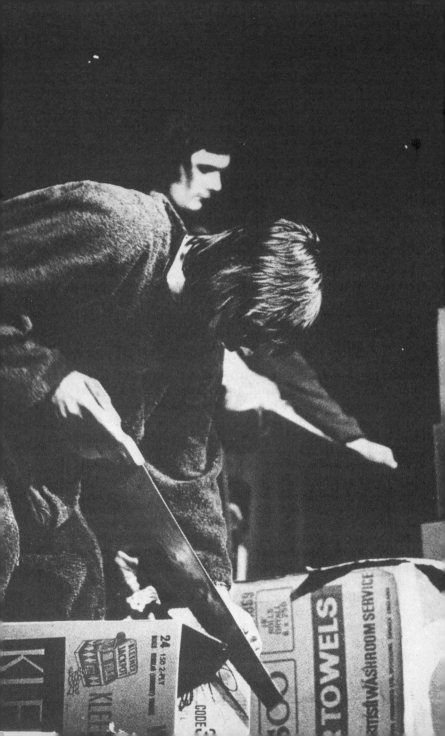

been destroyed in order to prevent the Russians from using it as an administrative centre; and we were told by a group of Americans that it was all the Russians' fault — Stalin had asked for the raid (a statement, incidentally, which there's no evidence to support). We could only say, 'But that's not how we see it. We've tried to show it as we see it.'

But at a country grammar school in Sussex, where I'd imagined the event would fail to entertain an audience of children from twelve upwards, the attention, from more than two hundred of them, was overwhelming in its intensity. None of them had heard of Dresden before, and statements that even to us had become commonplace brought physical gasps. The experience more than made up for the initial disaster in Bradford. It demonstrated to me that it was possible to communicate, simply and directly, very complex theatre statements to comparatively unsophisticated audiences.

The Destruction of Dresden was the last show we staged which was more of a happening than an entertainment. Events were, of course, still created. We staged the only American Presidential Election ever held in Bradford, and hired a real elephant as part of the event; Paul Binnaerts invented the building of the Union Pacific Railway at the Serpentine Gallery in London; Joe Dolan conceived the idea of painting a street in Bradford red, white and blue, and holding a tea-party there to celebrate the twentieth anniversary of the Coronation. But the work of the Theatre Group itself, which really came together seriously after the Dresden show, moved increasingly away from 'performance art' events, and in the direction of using popular entertainment idioms to make political statements.

It was in this sense that the Dresden project marked the culmination of one kind of work — and the beginning of another.

5. *'Each began, in his own way, to destroy cardboard boxes.'*

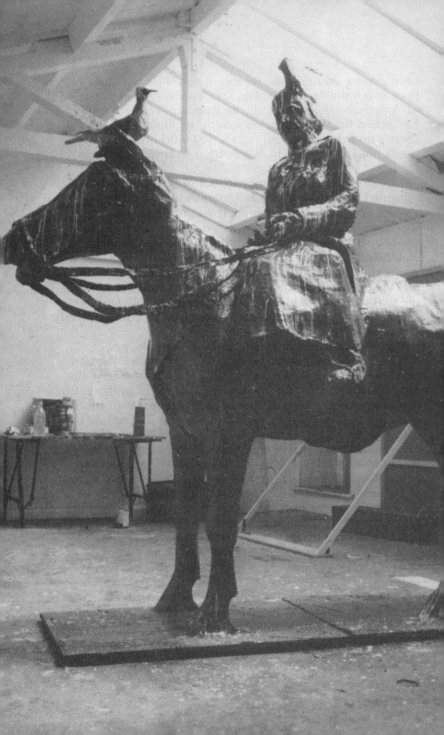

Chapter four
Passport to theatre

'From the first it has been the theatre's business to entertain people, as it also has of all the other arts. It is this
business which always gives it its particular dignity; it needs
no other passport than fun, but this it has got to have. The
theatre must in fact remain something entirely superfluous,
though this indeed means that it is the superfluous for
which we live. Nothing needs less justification than
pleasure.'

Bertolt Brecht, *A Short Organum for the
Theatre*

1

The most serious educational argument that could be level-
led against the structure of work that had been created at
the art college in the last few years was that it lacked continuity. Students normally only worked on complementary
studies projects for a fortnight a year. Attempts to structure
follow-up situations, in the shape of lectures, seminars or
workshop activities, only worked to the extent that the
students involved wanted to make them work — and not
because they had been written into the organization. In
spite of this, a good deal of follow-up work did take place.
It was impossible to organise an event like, for example, *The
Survivors* evening, without involving students long after the
fortnight's project was officially over. Other students had
formed groups to produce pamphlets; Adrian Mitchell's
students had organised poetry readings. The follow-up was
there when the students had become so involved in the
project that they themselves wanted to continue.

◀ *6. The Queen visits Bradford's Coronation Street, 1973.*

Most of the groups formed after particular projects kept together only until the work launched in the project had been finished. But one group in particular survived for a much longer period, providing a continuous thread to the work over a period of six years. This was the Theatre Group, the core of which stayed together, with backing from the Yorkshire Arts Association, Gulbenkian and the Arts Council, long after they'd stopped being students. The group eventually formed itself into a professional touring company, attached to the college, and was responsible for a body of work, which was presented successfully, not only all over Britain, but in several countries of Europe, including Poland and Yugoslavia, where the group won the major awards at the Zagreb Festival in two successive years.

The group had come together from a number of different projects. Some had been involved in the theatre workshop activities from the beginning. Some had never been to a theatre workshop, but had joined as a result of the *Hot Gospel* project, the Dresden project, and Adrian Mitchell's poetry workshops. Three had been members of the original Shrewsbury group. When they finished their diploma courses at the various colleges they'd gone to from Shrewsbury, they made their way to Bradford, to join in the work — one of them suddenly rang one day during the summer and said, 'I'm here.' One girl arrived from Manchester, where she'd done a psychology degree at the university, and asked if she could do some part-time teaching. Within a few months, she found herself playing in *John Ford's Cuban Missile Crisis.*

The group was formed by people who responded to each other's ideas and attitudes and inventions. We never sat down and hammered out an ideological line. But on the main purpose of the work, we all, instinctively, agreed.

We wanted, in the first place, to entertain people. We found the kind of theatre that tried to be 'literary', that pretended to create an illusion of 'real life', that was based on assumptions about 'motivation', and the inner feelings of naturalistically created 'characters', that depended primarily on speechifying, rather than on what *happened*, to be boring. We were determined to try and avoid being

boring, which meant that we would never let anything
through in our work which bored *us*. As well as not being
boring, we didn't want to be aggressive or violent or moral-
ly superior, either. We agreed with Brecht that 'theatre
needs no other passport than fun, but this it has got to
have.' 'Nothing,' added Brecht, 'needs less justification
than pleasure.'

At the same time, we wanted to entertain people by
appealing to their minds — to their wit, and intelligence,
and alertness. This didn't mean excursions into the realms
of high intellectual argument: the Marx Brothers appealed
to people's wit, and so did Morecambe and Wise. The early
Marx Brothers films, in particular, became models: we
liked the way every sequence was packed with gags. There
were so many that you could see the films several times,
and still pick up more. We wanted our shows to have that
kind of density. If people missed some of the information
at a first viewing, we preferred that — as long as they were
entertained — to the feeling that we'd underlined the
obvious.

We wanted also, however, to use this form of popular
entertainment to put forward for consideration ideas —
political, social, even philosophical — that concerned us.
We wanted to question accepted ideas about normality,
accepted attitudes towards both historical and contemporary events. And we wanted to question the accepted
attitudes, not only of our 'enemies', the political right, but
of our 'friends' on the left. We wanted, in fact, constantly
to re-examine our own attitudes. When we were dealing
with the Second World War, we tried to suggest that the
issues were not as simple as popular history made them out
to be — we drew on A.J.P. Taylor's *Origins of the Second
World War* — that the picture of Churchill as the great war
leader was not the whole truth, and that the parallel
between Eichmann and Harris was too close for comfort.
When we looked at the Cuban Missile Crisis, we tried, not
only to put the actions of the Kennedy brothers in a less
heroic and more realistic light, but also to question some
of the myths that had grown up around Guevara. I suppose
the ultimate in questioning assumptions was reached when

we made a play in which Hitler played the role of the
Messiah in the Oberammergau Passion Play — the popular
images of evil and good brought together in startling
relationship.

We wanted to find an idiom through which we could
handle these complex ideas while using forms that would
be popular and would make people laugh. For us, laughter
was a central political weapon. And so we turned increasingly towards the forms of entertainment that twentieth-
century audiences are familiar with. We made plays in the
style of movies, which radically affected the form of
theatrical presentation. We worked at discovering the
theatrical equivalent of the fluidity and pace of the Hollywood movies of the thirties and forties, which everybody
was now watching on television. This involved a great deal
of serious work on problems of *style* of performance, of
what was meant by acting, of the relationship of the actor
himself to the part he was playing. By continuously
switching roles, we emphasised the centrality of the performer as a person. In the Nixon show, for example (*The
Fears and Miseries of Nixon's Reich*, first performed in
February, 1974), one performer, Chris Vine, pretends to
be Nixon, pretending first to be Marilyn Monroe, then
Tony Curtis. Throughout all these switches, Chris Vine
remains himself, playing with a Yorkshire accent. But the
megalomaniac look in his eyes, and the thrust-out chin is
Nixon's. And the wiggle of the hips is Monroe's. We were
exploring, basically, a theatre of many dimensions.

And just as we played with the inter-relationship
between the performer and the role, we played with the
contradictions between word and object. 'You see this
bomb', Chris Vine would shout, waving a kettle. Your eyes
told you it was a kettle — the words and the actions of the
characters said it was a bomb. (But when we played that
scene in Poland, we made a cut-out bomb, and marked it
'Bomb' in Polish.) A great deal of the fun which we aimed
for was created by this use of props as playthings — which
stemmed right from the early 'anti-hero' workshop sketch.

Above all, we asked ourselves at every point, 'But is it
theatre? What's essentially *theatrical*? What couldn't be

◀   7. *'Using forms that would be popular . . . '*

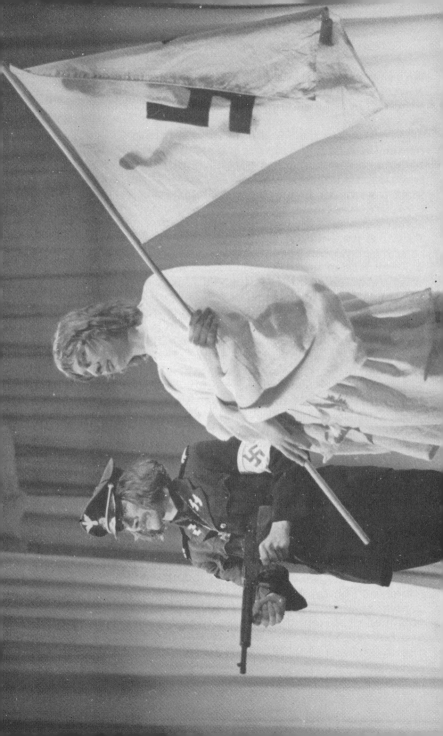

said in any other way?' A lot of the documentary plays
we'd seen — both in theatre and on television — might as
well have been pamphlets. Long chunks of information
were simply doled out in speeches; actions tended to be
merely illustrative ('he opened the door' — actor mimes
opening a door — 'and tip-toed into the room' — actor tip-
toes across stage). We tried never to put on to the stage
anything that could have been said, more simply, in
writing. Always, to us, theatre arose from contradiction —
between what you said you were doing, and what you were
actually doing, between what people saw, and what they
were told they were seeing, between the real performer,
physically *there*, and the parts he said he was playing.

The Theatre Group was a weapon forged to express a
collective attitude, which, in the words of Doug Lawrence,
made you 'see things, laugh at them — and manage them'.

2

The Theatre Group's first major show was commissioned
in the summer of 1968 by the National Association of
Mental Health for the Seventh World Congress of Mental
Health at Holland Park Comprehensive School in London.
Peter Brook had been originally approached, on the strength
of his *Marat/Sade* show, and asked to present an event
which, for one morning, would destroy the conventions of
an international conference, and present the delegates with
a direct, dramatic experience. He hadn't been available, and
he passed the commission on to us. Adrian Mitchell, who
had been one of the *US* team, worked with us on the
project.

From the start, we saw the commission as an opportunity
to present, not a series of arguments, but an alternative
way of thinking, feeling and behaving, to a group of people
for whom 'normality' was something to be taken for
granted, something towards which patients had to be led.
In thinking about the project, Adrian Mitchell and I spent
a lot of time trying to imagine a concept of reality which
would be completely different from the one held by progressive social psychologists. Suddenly, we hit on the idea

◀ 8. *'The popular images of evil and good brought together in startling
       relationship . . . '*

of the Old Testament world picture as one that had been accepted for thousands of years, but that was radically different from any contemporary attitude.

With the rest of the group, we created a show that used the Old Testament as a theme. At the foot of Mount Sinai, a group of anonymous Israelites — or were they mental patients? — played out, as dramatic therapy, their serious and painstaking attempts to comprehend the workings of the Almighty in their legends: Adam and Eve, Cain and Abel, the tower of Babel, Jonah. In a control tower above, surrounded by buttons marked 'Plague', 'Flood', 'Fire', a manic, pantomime God, accompanied by a liberal, ineffective Jesus ('Oh, look, Daddy,' he cries at the height of the Flood, 'there's a little lamb drowning'), and a sharply technologically-minded Holy Ghost (the Spook), dispensed random and unpredictable rewards and punishments.

'The impact of ideas,' wrote Catherine Itzin, the only critic there, 'was enormous. The impact of the drama in theatrical terms was also enormous.' She went on to point out that the importance of the show lay in the context — in the fact that it wasn't presented to an undefined audience in a theatre, but to a particular group engaged in a particular form of social action. We hadn't in any way tried to tailor a show for this particular audience. We had done and said exactly what we wanted. But we'd been aware that we weren't working in a vacuum, that we weren't trying to present a nebulous entertainment. We were playing inside a social situation for a sharply defined purpose. The situation contrasted strongly with the absence of such a context in the established theatre; two years earlier, working with Peter Brook on *US*, I'd been conscious that we weren't really talking to anybody in particular — that the Aldwych audience had no common core of interest to which our communication could be directed.

We ended the show by offering the audience of psychiatrists and social workers a choice between the Golden Calf — which offered gifts of red wine — and the tablets Moses had brought down from Mount Sinai. And we'd hoped to complete the dislocation of the sense of normality

by putting two camels in the school playground, for the
psychiatrists to encounter as they left the performance. The
camels never turned up.

It was the success of *Move Over Jehovah* that made us
all want to do more work together. We invented a hot
gospel show, *Looking Forward to 1942*, which told the
story of the Second World War in terms of a pentecostal
meeting. At the beginning of the show, the pentecostals
were totally free in their behaviour. They sang gospel songs,
praised the Lord, and had a good time, in the style of the
Glory meeting. But as the meeting — and the war — progressed, they became increasingly dependent on leaders, and
were reduced to puppets. A Churchill figure sat in the
middle of the stage, painting, throughout each performance,
a pretty pastoral painting — there are copies of Churchill's
posthumous paintings in pubs around Europe. The
believers jumped to his every whistle. At the end of the
show, a girl, made helpless by a blindfold, sang, 'Take myself, and I will be, Ever always all for thee', while rubble
was dumped, as an offering, all around her. As she sat
amongst the rubble, an evangelist invited the audience to
surrender their lives to Jesus, while the believers sang,
'Only believe'. The show, which had grown out of the work
we'd done on hot gospel, and on Dresden, and recording
people who had been bombed in Bootle during the war,
went to Amsterdam, where people told the members of the
group that it was Brechtian, and to Zagreb, where it picked
up all the prizes that were going. But the most satisfying
performance took place in a British Legion club in South
Wales, where the audience was initially very hostile, but
stayed discussing the show for several hours, and ended
round the piano singing, 'We'll meet again'.

The God show, and the 1942 show, were the first shows
in which the group mastered the techniques necessary to
make the ideas work in performance. But it was with *John
Ford's Cuban Missile Crisis* that the group discovered its
basic style.

John Ford's Cuban Missile Crisis was commissioned by
a group of left-wing students from Bradford University,
who gave us a free hand to prepare a new show as part of

the Lenin Centenary Celebrations in April 1970. We'd just
spent several months working on a show called *Quasar*,
based on Arthur Koestler's book about how astronomers
throughout history have imagined the universe — *The
Sleepwalkers*. We'd discovered a lot of images. Bernard
Lovell had turned up as a Lancashire comedian, holding an
umbrella upside down as if it were a radio telescope, and
saying, 'It always rains in Manchester'. A group had played
a game on stage with a huge ball, while an astronomer
tried to work out the orbit. And a scientist had explained
a number of theories about quasars, while a boy and a girl
had fought a Laurel-and-Hardy battle with custard pies
behind him. But somehow, the images had never come
together into a dramatic whole, and the show hadn't
worked in the end.

When we were asked to do a play to celebrate a revolutionary, we seized on the idea of the Cuban Missile Crisis,
because it had been in our minds for some time, because
it would involve examining what the Russian Revolution
had turned into, and how it affected a contemporary
revolution, in Cuba, but also because the story itself, un-
like *Quasar*, was essentially dramatic.

We had the idea from the start of telling the story as if
it were a western: Dean Rusk had himself used the language
of a western at the height of the crisis, ('We was eyeball to
eyeball, and I think the other fellow just blinked'). And
Norman Mailer, in *The Presidential Papers*, had seen
Kennedy as a film hero. 'Of necessity', he wrote, about
Kennedy's nomination for President, 'the myth would
emerge once more, because America's politics would now
be also America's favorite movie, America's first soap opera,
America's best seller.'

In the first rehearsal, we imagined two western heros
confronting each other. One threw down a broom, which
happened to be lying around, and said to the other, 'You
cross that line, Nicki, and I'll blow your brains out'. From
that moment, the broom became a central image in the
play — we presented U Thant, for example, as a little nig-
ger boy, sweeping the streets, who's suddenly made sherrif.

9. *'The broom became a central image in the play.'* ▶

'Do I get a gun?' he says, and Kennedy replies, 'No: use
your broom.'

At first, we conceived the western only as a general
image. But, as we worked, we became more specific. In
thinking about Kennedy himself, we thought increasingly
of one star in particular — Henry Fonda, with the liberal
goodwill and the solemn moralising, linked with ruthless
action. We thought of Fonda in such films as *My Darling
Clementine* and *The Grapes of Wrath*, and this led us
straight to the movies of John Ford. So we came to present
the Cuban Missile Crisis as if it were a movie being directed
by John Ford — with Henry Fonda as Jack Kennedy, Lee
Marvin as Nicki Krushchev, and Groucho Marx (out of
place in a John Ford movie, but right for the part) as
President Batista. We began by presenting scenes from old
Ford movies, then showed him making this film of the
Missile Crisis. But images from the past kept breaking in.
So, Kennedy's proclamation announcing the blockade was
part of a sequence from *They Were Expendable*, a film
about fighting the Japs in the Pacific, which was itself in
the style of a western. . .

One scene in particular demonstrated our way of working. I'd written an episode which demonstrated US inter-
vention in Cuba since the beginning of the century. But it
was all verbal, with the information being pushed out,
documentary-style, to the audience. We realised that the
scene wasn't working, so we sat down in a pub and asked
ourselves how we could relate the information to the western idiom. Somebody pointed out that we hadn't used a
cattle-rustling scene. So Ian Taylor went off and made
some cows. They were flat and two-dimensional and very
realistic; and they sat on the stage and stared out at the
audience. And we invented a scene in which the United
States became a cowboy trying to protect a girl (Cuba)
from a Mexican cattle-rustler. The rustler was branding the
cattle with an S, so the cowboy turned the S into a dollar
sign — and took the cattle to his own side of the stage. All
the information was kept in the scene — but it was trans-
formed into metaphor.

10. The broom again . . . ▶

Two other scenes summed up the show. In one, Ford rehearsed Fonda (playing Kennedy) in the proclamation speech. 'Now I want you to remember that this is the most important speech in the movie. It's possibly the most important in the history of mankind.' 'Yes, sir, thank-you, sir,' says Fonda, and rehearses it getting it all wrong — his gun looks too threatening, he waves his broom about, he grins in the wrong places. 'For God's sake, try and look *sincere,*' shouts Ford in despair. The scene captured all the complex relationships between play-acting and reality that were there in the crisis itself.

The second key sequence came at the height of the crisis. As Kennedy moved to confront Krushchev, whose ships were approaching the line, Ford intervened with his usual catch-phrase, 'That's well: print it.' 'That's not well,' cried Fonda/Kennedy. 'What do you think this is, one of your god-damned movies? We're gonna see this thing through.' History had overtaken the myth. The action might be that of the sherrif threatening to blow somebody's brains out: the results would have been world catastrophe.

We played *John Ford's Cuban Missile Crisis* in front of audiences ranging from students at the international festival in Zagreb, sophisticated theatre-goers at the Open Space Theatre, London, to parents and children in the hall of a village school just outside Huddersfield, and young people in a pub in Sunderland. What delighted me most about the play was the success it had with non-theatre-going audiences. We had, I felt, discovered a style that was both intelligent and ironic, and genuinely popular. When we played in the school-hall outside Huddersfield, a whole cross-section of the population turned out to see the show. The kids liked the cowboys, the old folk liked the music, and the ordinary adults in the audience re-lived the thirteen days of the crisis. Afterwards, parents were telling their children about the night the world nearly came to an end.

John Ford's Cuban Missile Crisis probably reached the widest audience of any of the shows we made. But in the years that followed, the Theatre Group, working some-times with students, and sometimes on their own, conti-nued to create shows that toured widely, in the United

◀ *11. 'So Ian Taylor made some . . . cows.'*

12. 13. *'Wilson's glorious retreat from socialism to Dunkirk.'*

Kingdom and in Europe. The year after the Missile Crisis, we invented, *James Harold Wilson Sinks the Bismarck*, a play in the style of British war films, depicting Wilson's glorious retreat from socialism to Dunkirk, a retreat which he claimed as an advance and a defeat which he hailed as a victory. The central scene showed Wilson leading the retreat. 'We're going to advance — but in order to fool the enemy, we're going to advance backwards. Benn: lay a minefield behind us. Forward — march.' As the group marched triumphantly backwards towards the rear of the stage, the Chairman of the Bank of England appeared, as a Nazi officer, holding a bomb. 'Herr Wilson: this bomb will explode at any moment. You must devalue the pound.' 'Never, you German Kraut,' cried Wilson. 'Men. About turn. Forward march.' 'Just a minute,' said Benn, 'I've laid a minefield behind us, and I don't know where the mines are.' 'What are you going to do, Herr Wilson?' shouted the Chairman of the Bank of England. 'Yes, what are you going to do, Harold?' shouted Alec Douglas-Home. 'Yes, what are you going to do?' shouted George Brown. 'Do?' said Wilson. 'I'll show you.' He marched back through the minefield unharmed. 'I'm going to devalue the pound.' Everybody cheered.

It was in *James Harold Wilson Sinks the Bismarck*, too, that we presented a picture of the Marxist world view of economics, in the style of a parody of Chinese street theatre. The scene involved us all in a great deal of research, and we argued for days about the arithmetic. The show never reached London: but it proved to be as popular with audiences round the country as the Cuba show had been. The most successful evening we had with the show was when we performed it at what should have been a Miners' Benefit during the 1972 strike: but that day the miners had just won their demands, and the evening turned into a victory celebration. I always wanted to present the show at the Labour Party Conference, but never succeeded in organising it.

Without doubt, the boldest intellectual idea the Theatre Group explored during these years was the one at the centre of *The Passion of Adolf Hitler*. We presented the life of Hitler in terms of the Oberammergau Passion Play, with Hitler himself playing the role of the Messiah. Some of the scenes, when they worked, were extremely powerful and disturbing. The Sermon on the Mount took the form of a Nuremberg rally: Hitler recited the parable of the talents to the Bankers of Dusseldorf — 'To him that hath shall be given, from him that hath not shall be taken away even that which he hath.' 'Very true,' said the Bankers. And Von Stauffenberg planted his bomb during the Last Supper — 'One of you shall betray me.' said Hitler, and Von Stauffenberg said, 'Lord, is it I?' By the end of the play, Goering, Himmler and Speer were competing for the role of Judas Iscariot, and Jesus had been tried at Nuremberg for the murder of the male children of Bethlehem. The play ended with Goebbels proclaiming the permanent revolution, as Hitler/Jesus was taken down from the cross.

One of the problems with the Hitler show was that of style. When we staged a western or a war film, the style imposed itself: but it was difficult to find a popular style for the Oberammergau Passion Play. We settled eventually for a style taken partly from Buñuel, and partly from pantomime.

Audiences in general found the Hitler show less accessible than the two earlier shows had been. They laughed — and then felt that they ought not to have been laughing. Once again, the most successful performance was given to a specialist audience — of Christian pacifists at a conference in Sheffield of the War Resisters' International. A German group there asked if they could have the script to take back to Germany.

I felt that in the Hitler show, the group had achieved a complexity of ideas and style that they hadn't reached before: but that its appeal was bound to be limited. We turned from Hitler to Nixon, and presented Watergate in terms of Billy Wilder's *Some Like It Hot*, as a battle between rival gangsters, representing the Democrats and the Nixon gang. We took as a starting point Chomsky's remark that, after what had happened in Vietnam and Cambodia, to try Nixon for Watergate was like trying Al

14. 'a style taken partly from Buñuel, partly from pantomime.'

15. 'Watergate . . . as a battle between rival gangsters.'

Capone for income-tax evasion. Theatrically, the show was probably the most effective we'd created. But by this time events in college were catching up on the group, and the show was never even performed in its final version.

During the seven years of its existence, the Bradford Art College Theatre Group had provided a focus for the varied work in education through theatre that was going on in the college. The group had demonstrated the possibilities of continuity in an open situation, and, in doing so, had entertained audiences of many different kinds, and had shown that theatre can be popular without dispensing with wit, irony, intelligence and mind.

And that, to me, was a point worth making.

3

In 1973, I wrote for the Arts Council a paper which summed up the conclusions about *Education Through Theatre*, which I'd drawn over the years at Bradford. I quote them here, because they seem to offer a summary of the ideas that informed all our work.

1.   The aim of education is to help people learn how to understand, control and, ultimately, change their environment. But the education system in this, and in most other advanced industrial societies, is geared to precisely the opposite end: i.e. pupils are taught that the world is extremely difficult to understand; that only a privileged few can reach such an understanding; that these few have the right to control the activities of all the rest; and that, far from trying to change their environment, the vast majority of people should try and fit in happily with the situation as it is. Education tries to teach people how to adjust successfully to the social role they'll be called on to play.

2.   The way in which this educational process works can best be seen by examining the *form* of education in our society. At the age of five, the child is herded by

law (in other words, by an undefined 'them') into an institution with other children of his age. The precise form the child's environment takes over the next eleven years will be decided by a group of 'experts' — teachers — who create that environment for him. The teachers are in power because they have acquired a particular kind of knowledge which is only open to the few. In the early stages of education, this knowledge has a wide application and is related to the obvious needs of the pupil: i.e. the pupil is taught reading and writing. As a result, the child can read the bubbles in comics and work out how much spending money he's getting — both useful skills. But as the pupil moves through the structure, the knowledge the teachers are supposed to be communicating becomes increasingly divorced from any immediate concrete use. By the time the child reaches the age of eleven, he is confronted with a whole world of mystification. Subjects, with mysterious, learned-sounding names, come at him in forty-minute slots. Algebra follows geography, chemistry gives way to French. . . . Nobody explains to the pupil why these particular areas of knowledge should be considered essential to his education — except that there are equally mysterious pieces of paper, called O- and A-levels, which are steps towards a higher place in society — a place similar to that occupied by the people who control the pupil's life. The pupil may not understand why he is learning quadratic equations: but one thing is clear — that it's the ability to do quadratic equations that gives the maths master his power in that particular environment. And so the right to make decisions, to control, to lead, is linked directly in the pupil's experience with the acquisition of what, to him, is mumbo-jumbo. Conversely, the inability to acquire this mumbo-jumbo means that you are in no position to understand or control your environment — or to make the vital decisions that affect your own life. This is one of the most powerful single lessons that our education system teaches.

3. But there are others. The 'experts', the teachers, spend
    their lives under the illusion that they are passing on
    to their pupils knowledge of their subjects. They think
    they're teaching maths and French. Yet any of us —
    even those of us who were successful in conventional
    academic terms — looking back on all those hours
    spent in classrooms, grappling at a terrifyingly elemen-
    tary level with subjects we've never looked at again
    since we left school, can only consider how *little* we
    learnt in all those hours. Knowledge acquired about
    any of these mystifying subjects before, at the very
    least, advance sixth-form level, is minute compared
    with the hours of organisation and control that go
    into teaching them. Until you realise that the organi-
    sation and control aren't about teaching subjects at
    all.
4. The organisation is about organisation. The pupils
    may not learn much Latin and maths; but they learn
    in concrete, experiential terms, that their lives are con-
    trolled by other people; that how they spend their
    time is dictated by a timetable prepared by 'them';
    that when bells ring they must drop whatever they are
    doing and do something else. They learn, too, that
    knowledge is fragmentary and unrelated to experience;
    that they are supposed to be equally interested in all
    branches of this knowledge; but not too interested,
    because the bell will go; and that if they are not
    interested, the teachers have the right to label them
    dull and stupid. In time, as the teacher of any D-
    stream will tell you, they begin to act out the role:
    they *become* dull and stupid. Inside this totalitarian
    structure, which controls the whole of your working
    life, there are odd contradictions. The civics master
    will explain to the school-leaving class that they live
    in a democracy, and that this means that they have
    the right to rule their own lives. But the pupil's con-
    crete experience over the last eleven years tells him
    much more forcibly that other people have the right
    to set up, organise and control his working environ-
    ment. For the most part, he will find this a fair re-

flection of the world outside, when he starts work in
a factory. (It probably never occurs to him that those
in apparent control are also controlled by the system
to which they belong: that even the man at the top,
the Prime Minister, will be warned by security about
who he oughtn't to sleep with.)

5. The sense of other people, with mysterious knowledge,
controlling your life is what our education system is
structured to communicate. The form of that communication is *theatrical*, ritualistic. The lining-up in
the playground when somebody blows a whistle; the
morning assembly, where power is displayed, often
decorated with theatrical emblems, such as gowns;
the rituals of moving from room to room when the
bell rings; all these are theatrical in their effect. That
is to say, they work in the way that theatre works,
making the abstract concrete, demonstrating in
physical terms where the power lies. Even a lesson is
theatrical, with the teacher playing a role in public.
Until we begin to understand that the education
system itself works in terms of theatre to communicate a particular experience of society, we won't get
very far in saying what the role of theatre — *our*
theatre, not the education system's — can be in contributing to the true aim of education, that of giving
pupils understanding, control, and the power to make
decisions about changing their environment.

6. It's easier, in fact, to see the way in which theatre —
our theatre — can be trapped into helping to bolster
up the system as it exists, rather than finding ways of
offering an alternative. In the first place, 'drama'
itself is increasingly seen as one more respectable subject on the timetable. In fact, many progressive
teachers of drama and film assert that their subjects
will only be taken seriously once they are examinable.
Such an argument, given the present situation, is
understandable, but undermines the role of the the
theatre in education as I understand it.

Secondly, the theatre itself, by emphasising its own
'professionalism', runs the risk of adding to the

mystique of the power of the expert. It is one thing
to insist that theatre-in-education work should be of
a high standard: it is quite another to talk about the
theatre profession as if a few years at a drama school,
however appalling, has initiated the actor into
mysteries the layman can know nothing of. The danger
is that theatre-in-education groups will actually *add* to
the pupil's sense that the world is a mysterious place
run by initiated people whose skills he can't hope to
acquire.

Thirdly, there's the danger that the theatre will
accept the role of yet another teaching aid. So: history
will be taught through theatre documentaries, civics
through plays about social problems. If the theatre
accepts this role, it will merely be confirming yet
again the pupil's awareness of the gap between the
apparent content of the lessons ('the meaning of
democracy'), and the real content — which is that an
undefined 'them' will draw the boundaries within
which the academic discussion can take place.

Fourthly, as older pupils begin to rebel against the
education that's been imposed on them from outside
(by staying away from school, or refusing to be disciplined in class) there's an increasing danger that the
teachers will use our theatre as, at best, sugar on the
pill, and, at worst, yet another form of oppression.
To perform a play, however good and well-intentioned,
to two hundred school-leavers, who have been
dragooned into a hall by teachers, who see the exercise as one more way of keeping reluctant young
people occupied for another afternoon of their lives,
is to experience first-hand an oppressive situation, and
to put the theatre at the service of the, themselves
oppressed, oppressors.

7. If this sounds negative, what it means is that we need
to go back and think again about the basic elements
of theatre, as well as about the basic elements of
education. Theatre is essentially a form of play. One
group of people (the actors) play at being another
group of people (the characters in the drama), for

the entertainment of a third group of people (the
audience).

Now the connection between play and education
has long been accepted, at least in theory. Very young
children first begin to learn through immediate experience: but soon the immediate experience no longer
satisfies the learning appetite, and so the children
invent wider, imagined situations, through play, so
that the range of learning can be extended. In the
early years of the primary school, 'progressive' infant
teachers recognise this process as valid, and continue
to encourage learning through play: but after a time
the school imposes its own rituals, its own theatrical
framework, and play is, for the most part, banished
from the learning situation.

But the element of play doesn't vanish. It goes
underground, and nobody takes it seriously any longer, but it remains. Children go on making their
dramas in the playground — dramas of cowboys and
Indians, ritual dramas of hide and seek, dramas about
spacemen and flying saucers. Later, they begin to
make more domestic dramas — the boys playing at
being pop stars, the girls playing at dressing-up to
attract the boys. Before going on a date, they rehearse
— i.e. they go over in their minds what they're going
to say to each other. They learn what they're going to
say by watching other people's games on television —
Hollywood movies, or *Top of the Pops*. All this is
outside the structured education given by the school:
the drama teacher will call them in from the schoolyard from a game involving an escape from an Indian
encampment, will put on a record, and ask the kids
to imagine they're trees.

8. The first positive step towards any theatre-in-education programme is to re-identify theatre with play,
and play with learning. School has pushed play out
into the schoolyard. The theatre must put play back
at the centre of experience. This means taking all
forms of play and entertainment more seriously than
what the school sets up as serious. If we have to say

which is more educational, preparing for French dictation, or watching Laurel and Hardy, we shall say watching Laurel and Hardy. Nothing, says Brecht, needs less justification than pleasure, and play needs to be seen as a positive value in its own right. But it's also a tool. In play, as in theatre, the abstract is made concrete. Young children learn elementary geometry by playing with shapes. There's no reason why the complexities of relativity, or economics, or international politics, shouldn't be explored through play — as Kurt Vonnegut explores the destruction of Dresden by playing at science fiction. But it's the play itself — the imaginative processes involved, and the concrete way in which these processes express themselves — that matters above all. By demonstrating the importance of play, the theatre is also demonstrating an alternative way of looking at social processes — alternative, that is, to the way the school looks at them, for the school has made them marginal. At one end of the scale, the play can be extremely simple theatre — as when school-children play at imitating their teachers. At the other end of the scale is Brecht, who, in *Arturo Ui*, plays at gangsters while making a play about Hitler.

9. In putting play, and entertainment, at the centre of the learning process, the theatre challenges the present educational system. But that system itself is not monolithic. The teachers, too, are trapped in the oppressed-oppressor role, and those who want to escape find ways of doing so. By reinstating play, the theatre can enlist the help of teachers looking for ways out, and offer them the possibility of playing a part in the invention of alternative learning situations. These learning situations are linked with theatre at a basic level — but they're hardly what the theatre establishment, or bodies like the Arts Council, would recognise as professional theatre performances. One's tempted to say, 'so much the worse for the Arts Council', except that, as Joan Littlewood puts it, 'kids playing games on street-corners are great, but some-

body, sometime, has got to think seriously about how
what we've learned from these games can be turned
back into effective theatre'. And here, perhaps, we're
coming near to the truth of the situation. For it's
always assumed that the 'theatre' has a lot to teach
young people that the schools aren't teaching; but
perhaps a more reasonable assumption would be that
young people have a lot to teach the theatre about
theatre. In straight theatre terms, two of the most
entertaining performances I've ever seen were i) a
show about the bombing of Coventry, put together
in the form of *Have a Go, Joe* by Gordon Vallins and
a group of young people in Coventry; and ii) a version
of *A Midsummer Night's Dream*, performed by com-
prehensive-school children, using football chants and
a trad jazz band. Both these productions had the
essential quality of play that's largely been lost in our
theatre — and that we might well begin to re-learn by
looking at what the playground culture has to offer,
and bringing it back into our theatre.

10. It would, however, be a mistake to narrow down a
discussion about theatre and education to a discussion about theatre and schools. For, increasingly, we're
beginning to realise that education doesn't end with
schools, that what is important is that people should
go on learning throughout their lives, at all ages. And
if this is true, then the importance of theatre as an
alternative form of learning situation, and an alternative way of looking at society, becomes even greater.
In some places, the concept of the age-based school
is beginning to give way to the idea of learning situations based on community interests and involving
people of all ages, children, young people and adults.
A theatre company involved in such situations, and
committed to learning through imaginative play
activity, could use their skills to become part of the
learning situation — taking part in research, setting up
demonstrative sessions, or improvisations, or game
situations to help common understanding, and, above
all, preparing performances that would be linked with

a particular situation, and would be at the service of
a particular audience. (An example of this particu-
larised kind of drama activity was our own show,
Move Over Jehovah, which we specially prepared for
a particular community, a World Congress of Mental
Health, working on the preparation with psychiatrists,
social workers and even mental health patients.) It
may be, in fact, that if we're thinking about theatre
in education at all, we ought to abolish the category
of 'Youth Drama' as obsolete: and begin to think
more carefully about the place of theatre in a community of all ages.

Such a company would draw its strength from working
inside a meaningful context. Neither the content nor the
style of its work would be dictated by the community to
which the company belonged: but the work would be made
for and offered to a specific group of people sharing
specific interests.

A company of this kind would inevitably become involved with the educational and social struggles of the community which it served: but it must not be allowed to
become one more social service. Its only reason for existing
would be to make theatre — theatre that has re-discovered
the joy of play, and found a meaningful context to play in.
The Theatre Group had, in the first place, grown out of and
belonged to the college community. But by the time of
Move Over Jehovah, *Looking Forward to 1942* and *John
Ford's Cuban Missile Crisis* the group had grown beyond
the college situation.

An imaginative local education authority would have
realised that something had come out of the college that
could make a unique contribution to community education. By 1970, the opportunity was there to create a
genuine community theatre in Bradford, home-produced,
working in a popular style, actively contributing to the life
of the area.

I proposed that the group should be officially attached
to the college, should work for half its time as a touring
group, and for the other half of its time on projects in
Bradford; and should be supported, half by the local autho-

rity and half by the Arts Council.

Unfortunately, imagination was not a quality in great evidence at Bradford City Hall. The support was forthcoming from the Arts Council, from the Yorkshire Arts Association and from Gulbenkian — but not from the local authority. The group was increasingly forced to turn itself into one more touring fringe theatre company, and became increasingly separated from the work of the college.

The proposal to attach the group to the college was not in any way outlandish. The Coldstream report had encouraged art colleges without Dip.A.D. to become more involved with community activities, and the college had actually taken over an Adult Education Department, which was now being directed by a former colleague of mine from Shropshire, Arthur Arnold.

The authority was always on the point of helping us. But the help never came. One by one, experienced actors drifted away from the group. Two of them, who had been in at the beginning in Shrewsbury, were offered lucrative jobs in other departments.

By the summer of 1973, only a hard core of four remained. But by this time the future of the group had become entangled with developments that were to bring Bradford's experiments in alternative education to an end.

Chapter five
Discovering the
limits of freedom

they called a meeting
and invited us to sit round the table
so we listened to city architects
unsmiling and smartly dressed
they slowly explained
in Bradford accents
the functional qualities
of this threepenny bit building
illustrated on a piece of paper
supposedly a new art college
it wasn't very nice
it didn't please me
and when they found out
what we wanted
— underground tunnels
and transparent domes
zeppelins in the sky
and a nearness to the sea
they were amazed
and admitted speechlessness
and someone said
it would cost too much
what a nasty thought

Veronica Hussey: Bradford student

'It's really simple: but for that reason, like all simple things, so difficult to achieve.'

Bertolt Brecht

1

The developments which led to the castration of the work by 1974 were largely political and administrative. But as early as 1970 important educational problems had begun to appear. They were problems which arose naturally out of extensions of the work: and they are worth discussing in some detail because they are likely to confront anyone engaged with the work of creating freedom in education. In our case, they were thrown into focus by the establishment, in 1970, of a full-time college diploma course in our area of work.

The course — which had originally been proposed by members of the Theatre Group, but which, ironically, was only launched after the proposers had left — was known as Film/Theatre/Television. Film and Television were included, partly for political reasons — they were recognised by the bureaucracy as 'visual arts', and that was what art colleges were supposed to be about — but mainly because I felt the time had come to extend the methods developed in our theatre work into other media.

We had, as I saw it, two principal aims: first, to extend the concept of theatre, as a concrete element in the educational situation, to include film and television — and to produce films and television programmes in the process; and, secondly, to extend the idea of fortnights of freedom based on common interest into the realisation of permanent freedom.

Both aims produced problems — as we were to discover as soon as we started the first year's work.

2

The first problem arose quite simply from the act of advertising a course. As both the Theatre Group and I had imagined it, a full-time course would provide a way in which people who had discovered, through working together, that they shared a common commitment, would be able to pursue that commitment single-mindedly without pretending that they were really doing Textiles or Advertising. In other words, the full-time work would have grown naturally out of an already functioning working-situation.

As soon, however, as we announced Film/Theatre/ Television as an alternative to Textiles or Advertising, we had students wanting to enrol, not because they were committed to a particular way of working, but because they found this alternative rather more attractive than any already offered. That first group which enrolled included one boy who rather liked taking photographs, but didn't want to go and work in the graphics department; one who was mad about motor-bikes; one who was interested in building complex recording machines; and one who was simply using the course as a way of working for John Fox's Welfare State. If they had shared any kind of common involvement, they could have brought their individual skills to a collective concern: but, in practice, all they really had in common was that they happened to have enrolled on our course. Later, we were to have students enrolling because they wanted to be 'actors', or to crash the TV play-writing market, or because they saw the course as a refuge for Fine Art drop-outs. The dilemma was this: that if we accepted students who weren't committed to our way of working, then any extension of that way of working became difficult; but, on the other hand, if we demanded such an initial commitment, then we were inventing our own entry qualifications — and our educational thinking rejected the very concept of entry qualifications. In the event, we accepted virtually anybody who wanted to come — though we always tried to spell out to prospective students what we thought we were about.

The second problem arose from the nature of the media we were now trying to explore. The joy of the theatre work had been that, by working in an old warehouse with eight people and a heap of junk, it had been possible to produce theatre that had to be taken seriously — that was 'real'. But with the rudimentary equipment that we always had it was impossible to produce a television image that *looked* like 'real' television. All we ever had was the equivalent of rough sketches for final ideas, which needed resources we didn't have to turn into finished products.

This problem need not have been crippling. It would have been possible, I argued, to produce such strong ideas that they would have come through in spite of the technical limitations. But it was linked with another, which existed mainly in the mind. The students — and not only the students, but experts we brought in, and schoolchildren and community groups we worked with — turned out to have a very deep-rooted concept of what 'real' television should be like. 'Real' television was what happened on the BBC and Yorkshire Television — and what they wanted to learn was how to make programmes that looked like that.

This was, of course, in total contrast to the attitude of the Theatre Group. When we'd started working in theatre, nobody had assumed that what we were aiming to do was to produce plays that looked like those that were being put on at the provincial reps or in the West End. We took it for granted that what we created would be *better* — more exciting, more full of ideas, more *funny*. Several members of the group had never been to the theatre in their lives: they never worried about breaking the rules because they didn't know what rules there were to break. Those of us who had been previously involved in the theatre wanted only to change it.

It was such an attitude that I had in mind when, in the original blurb to our course, I wrote loosely that we wanted to give opportunities to people who wanted to produce, direct, write, perform, and that the work they did might lead to possibilities of work in the various media. I had every reason at the time for believing this to be true: there were already record companies interested in our work, local radio seemed on the point of dramatic expansion, there were going to be increasing demands for the use of television and video in the education industry. There was no reason why we shouldn't create an alternative television in the way an alternative theatre and an alternative education structure had been created — and this in itself would lead to changes which would open up new possibilities.

But all this depended on the creation of work. We were setting out, ambitiously, to change the media — but this could only be done by the same kind of imaginative approach that we'd brought to the theatre work.

In other words, we weren't in the business of teaching people how to write Wednesday Plays or make left-wing versions of *Panorama*. But, as the course developed, this was increasingly what students were asking us to do. And we'd begun by trying to create a structure which would respond to the needs of the students . . .

3

The contradictions of the situation begun to emerge early in the course. We'd begun, gaily enough, by taking virtually all the recruits — all those who wanted to go — with the Theatre Group to an international seminar on documentary theatre in Rotterdam. I imagined that this would offer as concrete an introduction as possible to what we were about.

The trip created one of those dramatic situations on which a lot of the work in the last few years had been based. Most of the students involved were what would usually be described as 'non-academic'. They came from local schools, had few academic qualifications, had spent a couple of years in college, and had done one or two of our projects. None of them had any experience of universities and their methods.

One had survived at college the previous year by running a pig-farm. He'd been up every morning at five to deal with the pigs, and had rushed off every afternoon at tea-time to get back to his farm. He'd done this to make a basic living, since he got little or no grant. He'd also driven a milk-lorry — apparently without bothering to have a licence. The local bobby — whom he'd thought of as a mate — had turned him in; and rather than pay the fine he'd just spent several weeks in prison. It wasn't too bad inside, he said, once you'd got used to it.

One morning at Rotterdam a group of German university Marxists led a discussion in which they described how they'd made a documentary play explaining to the workers how the proletariat was exploited; how they'd tried to perform this for workers, but nobody seemed interested; and how this was because the workers had been brain-washed by the capitalist-controlled media. That afternoon, I noticed that the pig-farming student wasn't there: and neither was our expensive UHER tape-recorder. Later in the evening I ran into him and asked him where he'd been. 'Talking to bloody workers', he said. He'd taken the tape-recorder on a pub-crawl round the Rotterdam docks and recorded Dutch sailors singing 'It's a long way to Tipperary' . . .

These students were lively, down-to-earth, friendly. But they didn't really exist as a group at all. They would work together for a week or two on a project, but would then drift off on their own enterprises. The result was that there was no collective development.

This was demonstrated in the first project we did together with the newly-acquired video equipment — two Sony cameras, two small monitors, one large monitor and a mixer.

The project was one I'd initiated, but they were all happy to work on it. It was supposed to be about Nelson and Trafalgar — during a summer holiday with my family I'd found a trip round the Victory a very Brechtian experience, with the ship as a concrete image of the class divisions of the period. But the project was really about how we could use the new equipment to create the kind of images we'd been inventing in the theatre work.

As a one-off project, it was very successful. The students taught themselves how to use the cameras and the mixer. One student demonstrated the tactics of the Battle of Trafalgar by using salt cellars and vinegar bottles on a table. At the climax of the battle, he knocked over a vinegar bottle — and we cut, quickly, to another student, hamming the death of Nelson on a ship we'd built at one end of the studio out of old junk. As a visual image, the ship worked very well: it was non-realistic, but very simple and clear, and offered the hint of a workable television language that didn't depend on elaborate and expensive naturalistic sets.

Again, there was a scene in which Nelson built his own column out of tea-chests — 'It will be called Trafalgar Square; and there will be four bronze lions' — scrambled on top of his column, put a cardboard tube to his blind eye, spied on Emma philandering with the Prince Regent, and was then called down by the Prime Minister, and ordered to go and fight the Battle of Trafalagar. We didn't write a shooting script, but pointed the two cameras, from the front, at the action, to create a cardboard cut-out, two dimensional effect, and shot the scene as if we were recording a sporting event.

Most successful of all was a sequence in which a girl, Veronica Hussey, played Fanny Nelson as Fanny Craddock conducting a cookery demonstration. We'd discovered a recipe for 'basting a Spanish man o'war', and Veronica read out this recipe as she mixed up the ingredients, and then cooked them over a bunsen burner. Again, we used the cameras as outside broadcast units. Later Veronica Hussey wrote a poem describing this piece of work:

> played at being fanny nelson
> making a dish for horatio
> i gradually became involved
> and i was happy cracking eggs
> sifting flour
> adding margarine (gently)
> but best of all i liked
> chucking in dried peas
> and sloshing milk
> and i forgot i was on
> the video

The sense of play captured in the poem was one on which I hoped that the television work would be built. It was demonstrated again two years later by Veronica herself and another girl, Catherine Ann Whiteley, a beautiful blonde, who made a piece of video in which Cathy dressed up in an old-fashioned striped bathing-costume and a straw hat, and mimed Maurice Chevalier's 'Thank heaven for little girls' to a Veronica in pig-tails, sucking an ice-lolly and paying no attention to the song. The sequence, which they offered as part of their diploma show, was very funny: but, significantly, it was virtually a by-product — Veronica's main commitment for a year had been towards producing a book of poems, and the two of them had originally invented the sketch as part of a theatrical evening of nostalgic entertainment, and not as a result of exploring the

16. Veronica Hussey plays at being Fanny Nelson.   ▶

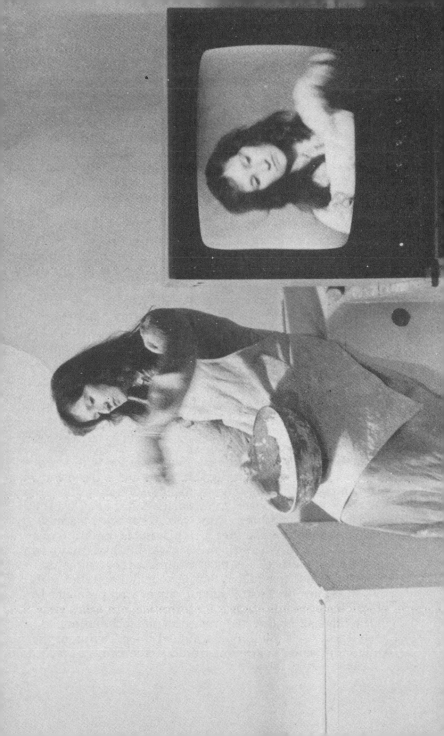

television medium. All the 'serious' television programmes offered by the students consisted of derivative documentaries about terraced houses and motorways.

What had happened, after that first project, was that there had been no collective follow-up in exploring the medium, or its possibilities. The students had developed their own individual concerns in several directions, but their general approach to television had been the simple one of 'Show us how to do it' — how to write a shooting script or set up an interview like 'they' did, 'they' being the professionals of the TV industry. Being friendly, they would humour me for an afternoon when I suggested playing games with the equipment — setting up, for example, a chat show in which the aim of the speaker was always to be in camera when he spoke, but the aim of the cameraman was never to show anybody that was speaking. Everybody would agree that such a game was very enjoyable — but then they would want to get back to a 'real' subject and 'real' techniques.

The problem was that once these 'real' techniques had been acquired, they limited in themselves the possibilities. For example, a member of the Theatre Group, Ian Taylor, had written a play about an industrial accident. In spite of the apparent solemnity of the subject, it was, in fact, a funny play, and demanded the simple, direct, cartoon-style acting we'd first developed in *The Happy Haven*.

Ian Taylor and a group of students worked with a professional producer at turning this script into a television play. As they built the set, put together the shooting script and rehearsed the moves, the students felt that at last they were learning something. They were. They were learning how to turn an original idea into a passable imitation of a Wednesday Play. When the project was finished, they had by far the smoothest and most complete programme the department had produced. But personally I couldn't feel that the course was really solving any central problems by producing poor imitations of a form that was dead, even in the original. I suggested that, now the techniques had been learnt, we should look again, with Ian Taylor, at the same script, and experiment with different ways of recording it. We did, in fact, spend one morning working on the opening sequence, and the work seemed to me to be promising: but, naturally enough, the students felt they'd 'done' that piece of work, and wanted to go on and make another programme just as 'professional'.

Another example of the way the urge to make 'professional' television led to the diminution of imaginative ideas was offered by a piece of work that was done on the subject of the Kronstadt mutiny, with the playwright, Trevor Griffiths. The working situation seemed one of the most promising we could create. Trevor Griffiths had worked in television, and therefore qualified as a 'professional'. But, on the other hand, he'd left TV to become a writer. He'd been half-commissioned by the National Theatre to work on this script, and he saw the project as an opportunity to try out a number of ideas. At the same time, a member of the Theatre Group, George Dorosz, was running a Theatre Workshop with another group of students as part of the complementary studies programme. This group would produce images for the Kronstadt programme.

George Dorosz had already demonstrated, with a group of day-release printing apprentices, a possible approach to video. Using the cameras, as we had done, as if they were recording a sporting event, he and the apprentices had invented a game based on the ritual of 'I'm the King of the Castle'. The King sat in a chair; the group lined up in single file. Each person in the file, in turn, had to invent a way of murdering the King and taking his place. Each murdered King had to invent a different way to die. The last King killed himself.

The images of death produced by the group were hammy and funny and exaggerated, but also, because of the ritual and the repetition, very strange. And when George Dorosz came to work on an image for the Kronstadt rising, he again took a game situation.

There was an episode in the Kronstadt story in which, paradoxically, the revolutionary Red Guards were given the job of preventing freezing and hungry peasants from taking wood to make fires from a pile outside the barracks. George Dorosz took the game in which one person faces a wall, while the rest of the group try and creep up and touch him, without being seen. The person facing the wall swings round suddenly and unexpectedly. If he sees you moving, he sends you back to start again.

In the Kronstadt version of this, the guard was facing the wall, and there was a pile of wood between him and the people who were creeping up. Their aim was to steal wood from the pile; but if the guard caught them, instead of sending them back to start again, he shot them with a wooden rifle, and they fell dead. By the end of the game, the room was full of dead bodies: they were people who were obviously students, but they wore scarves and old coats and worn-out boots over their student gear.

The game was, at first, recorded as it happened in the studio. As the peasants died, the cameraman instinctively zoomed in to the bodies to select the significant details — the scarves or the coats or the boots. The actual shooting was done ritualistically, and again the repetition created a very powerful and disturbing image. What made the sequence work was that it remained, very obviously, a game being played by students in a studio — and yet in their manner of playing, the students were offering their own physical comment on the events with which the programme was dealing: they were communicating a precise image of what had happened, and demonstrating also the contradictions of the situation. For the guard too was cold — he showed it by the way he buttoned his coat and beat with his arms.

The sequence worked: but it was in a different style from the rest of the 'programme'. The students who were making the programme decided that the way to solve the problem would be to film the sequence out of doors, in a more convincing location, and then cut the film sequence into the TV programme. They chose a quarry, taking care to keep out of the picture pylons, electric wires, cars. It was a bitterly cold afternoon, so there was no need for the players to pretend. There was a long-shot of 'peasants' coming over a hill, and then the students played the game in the quarry, dying in the mud.

When we eventually looked at the piece of film, all the

qualities which had made the original so extraordinary had gone. The students looked as if they were trying to be peasants and hadn't quite made it; the background looked like a location job done on the cheap; and the clear, ritualistic and demonstrative elements were no longer there. The result was a rather uninteresting piece of celluloid.

This inability to escape from accepted definitions of the media affected most of the television work in the course. For example, the same group who had worked on the Kronstadt project worked on a video programme called *Champion Jack Dupree in Halifax*. The subject had a lot of potential. Champion Jack was one of the old New Orleans blues singers. He had married a Halifax girl, and they lived in a council house in Halifax. Virtually ignored in Yorkshire, he made a living by playing and singing in Munich and Berlin.

Champion Jack turned out to be as great a performer in video interviews as he was with audiences. He was a natural — all you had to do was switch on the camera, and he'd describe to you how he was in a shop near the Chicago garage at the time of the St Valentine's Day massacre.

We set up an evening in which he performed at a local pub, while we recorded him. The pub was, he said, one of his regular haunts. He performed for several hours to two of our cameras as if they belonged to the BBC. His wife sat drinking with friends and listening in another corner. The Friday night regulars in the pub virtually ignored what was happening: they stood around the bar, talking and drinking through the great blues classics. As soon as Dupree finished, one of them took his place at the piano and sang 'I Believe'.

The event offered all the visual material for a precise comment on the whole situation: Dupree even sang a blues he'd written about the isolation of his existence in Halifax. And the evening itself was a concrete image of isolation.

But the group was obsessed with the idea of making a programme that would look like a sequence from one of the popular music shows on the channels. What mattered was the lighting, the number of different close-ups and angles that could be got of Dupree at his piano, the fades

and the superimpositions. The result was a competent
enough record of Dupree singing songs: but a failure to
match up to the possibilities of the situation.

Nothing could have more clearly demonstrated the
limitations of this 'professional' approach than an experience which was a spin-off from this project. A record company was interested in producing an LP of any sound-tapes
we might get about Dupree in Halifax. The students concentrated on producing a tape of songs, which sounded
roughly like an inferior recording of any other LP, and
they dressed it up with a 'professional' looking sleeve. But,
of course, the company wasn't interested in another set
of Dupree's songs: they were looking for something that
might have extended the idea of what was 'commercial'.

This urge to imitate the accepted was not confined to
the students. When, for example, a student called Simon
Haines — who was one of the most outspoken opponents
of this pseudo-professional approach — simply took the
television equipment to groups of twelve and thirteen year
old schoolchildren, and handed over the hardware without
any restrictions at all, he found that, invariably, for the
first session the children would be lost, not knowing where
to point the camera or how to get a picture in focus; that
in the next few sessions, when the basic techniques had
been mastered, the children's imagination would run riot
and produce a breathless stream of images; but that, by the
third day, they would be composing pictures, which looked
just as banal as any on *Calendar* or *Play School* or *Panorama*,
A typical group which I saw produced a set of stream of
consciousness images on the first afternoon which were
sharp and playful and funny. A boy pretended to be Mick
Jagger. His walk turned into the walk of a cowboy. Another
boy jumped in and confronted him. They walked together
like heroes out of a western. As they met, the confrontation turned into a fight on the floor. Another boy leapt
in with a microphone and announced, 'Saturday afternoon,
World of Sport: International Wrestling'. Both fighters
began to imitate wrestlers — one looked up from the fight
and said, 'Bring that camera in closer, I want to show how
it hurts. . .' Two afternoons later, the same group recorded

a sequence in which they all sang a song.The camera pan-
ned expertly down the line and zoomed in to a close-up of
a guitar, as they all chanted sweetly, 'I want to teach the
world to sing in perfect harmony. . .'.

What we discovered, in our work with television, was
the extent to which the concept of the 'norm' of television
stifles the imagination. On occasions, students, in occasional
pieces of work, threatened to escape. A group of schoolchildren one afternoon recorded an improvisation in which
they were pretending to be the IRA tarring and feathering
a girl informer. The girl was 'acting', pretending to scream
and be frightened, until someone poured real ink over her
face. For a fraction of a second she stopped and registered
real alarm — then accepted the discomfort as part of the
game, and went on with the 'acting'. But that moment of
uncertainty, which the camera recorded, was much more
'real' and immediate than any number of *Panorama* on-the-
spot films from Belfast. The game and the camera had
created a true and startling moment of Brechtian alienation:
it made you see a familiar phrase like 'tarring and feathering'
in a new, direct way.

Again, the student who had recorded workers in
Rotterdam, made a video programme which used the concept of television itself as a starting point. 'Television' was
an alien intelligence which invaded Bradford. Its natural
state was to show wavy lines on a screen. But human beings
had captured television sets and forced them to reproduce
pictures of other human beings. The programme showed
television sets imprisoned in shops, being stared at by
children and eventually liberated. Jeff Bennet was using
the medium itself as the basis of a story. (The difficulty
was that he was working very much in isolation from other
students: he wrote the script, recorded the images, and
spoke his own commentary; the programme would have
been stronger if it had been the product of collective
talents.)

The idea of an alien intelligence was taken up by two
members of the Theatre Group, Keith Knowles and Chris
Vine, in a project they did with sixteen-year-old school-
leavers. They took the camera into the streets and pre-

tended that they were alien beings asking questions of the camera. 'What's that?' they would say, pointing to a girl walking past — and the cameraman would quickly have to pick up the girl and then describe on the sound-track what it was we were looking at. The questioning was always slightly ahead of the picture, and both the pupils who provided the soundtrack description and we, the audience who later saw the images, were looking at the familiar through strange eyes.

All these, and many similar, pieces of work raised interesting possibilities. But they tended to exist in isolation. Whereas the Theatre Group had sustained an approach to both content and style over a number of years, the television work was fragmented. What was needed was a group which would work systematically on solving the problems that were being thrown up, and on exploring new problems.

But the creation and the keeping-together of such a group proved to be beyond the capacity of a course which was struggling with the even more fundamental problems of how to maintain a corner of freedom in a basically unfree environment.

5

Although I, personally, saw the development of the theatre work, and its extension into other media, as a central commitment, and the area where, as an individual, I had most to offer, I also believed that the course in general was as much concerned with the establishing and maintaining of a state of educational freedom as with the exploration of any particular areas of work. Not that I saw the two objectives as in any way separate or contradictory. The high quality of the work produced through the complementary studies programme and the Theatre Group had resulted directly from the creation of a structure in which people could come together freely on topics of common interest. I believed that if this concept of people working freely together could be extended into a full-time course, then the work would develop in directions which I couldn't foresee.

To a certain extent this happened: when we started the course, we never, for example, imagined that one girl would end by writing and printing her own book of poems; or that another student, Simon Haines, would spend most of his final year buying a house to set up a free school. But there were other students, who, because of the lack of compulsion in the situation, came to spend a lot of time in the coffee bar, dreaming of what they might do if only things were different. To me, real freedom had always meant more than the right not to do anything; it meant discovering what you could do and exercising your right to do it.

The point was emphasised, by a project directed by a former international footballer, Jimmy McIlroy, working, for the most part, with fifteen-year-old pupils from school, and apprentices of a local football club. We'd first contacted McIlroy when we were doing a project in which we recorded footballers talking about their job; but he turned out to have interesting ideas about education.

He believed, for example, that you wouldn't teach football, but that you could set standards and demand people reached them; and then when they did, you could set others. At Burnley, he said, he'd spent hours, practising centring a ball on to the head of a forward running at full speed in such a way that the forward would hit the ball just right without checking in his run. (When he went to play with another club, they asked him if he had any ideas to use in training, and he told them of this one. They had five internationals in the forward line at the time, but said it was too difficult. . .)

When Jimmy McIlroy spent a morning with a local club's apprentices — we were filming the session, which was the excuse for having him over — he found that they were being left on their own, in 'freedom', to run round the park and do a bit of 'ball-training'. He invited them to practise hitting the crossbar from fifteen yards. At first, they couldn't do it: but as the morning progressed, they became more and more skilful. After a couple of hours, they were hitting the bar regularly: and they were enjoying demonstrating a newly-acquired skill. It seemed to me that the apprentices had added to their freedom in a morning's concentrated work — whereas the students who were dreaming in the coffee bar were constantly limiting their own freedom: each project they didn't carry out meant a narrowing-down of their possibilities.

To me, true freedom came at the point when you were so on top of what you were doing that you could begin to enjoy it and play with the situation. Watching Chris Vine master a part in a Theatre Group performance was always to understand what this kind of freedom was about. Chris Vine was very inventive, but had great difficulty in learning words. The parts he played seemed increasingly to demand that he learn words. Always in rehearsal we went through the same process: in the early improvisations, Chris Vine would be wild and anarchic and responsible for many of the ideas; then he would start to learn to reproduce what he'd done, and we'd go through a stage where every rehearsal would keep stopping and starting. Then he'd just about get there, and turn in a few performances which were right, but all buttoned up. And then, suddenly, while remaining true to the text he'd cut loose, like a jazz soloist taking off — and that was freedom.

We spent a lot of time in the course trying to map out, through action, the boundaries of freedom. Was freedom threatened, for example, by the insistence of the administration that the students should 'sign-in' every morning and afternoon? Since the 'signing-in' could be easily circumvented, it seemed to most of us a waste of energy to stage a confrontation on such an issue.

Again — should we draw the line at producing an end-of course diploma show? We were all against 'examinations' and 'diplomas', but the only way students could get grants was by working for a 'College Diploma'. So we staged diploma shows and gave diplomas to anybody who actually offered any work of any kind. And Simon Haines offered, as his diploma show, an allotment attached to his free school, and forced the assessors to tramp thrugh mud to see it.

17. 'like a jazz soloist taking off . . . ' ▶

Again, how far was 'freedom' compatible with a planned programme in which everybody was required to take
part? 'Required', not in the sense of being compelled, or
ordered, but in the sense that, in expressing a commitment
to the course by enrolling for it, they were 'contracting',
voluntarily, to make the course work. And, since at first
the numbers were so limited, and since much of the media
work inevitably involved groups of people working together,
and since equipment was in such short supply, the only
way the course *could* be made to work, the only way, for
example, that projects which might open up new possibilities could be laid on, was if people agreed to make some
collective commitment, even if their own concerns and
interests weren't directly engaged. And yet — the high
quality work had, in fact, grown out of a total personal
commitment, and not out of the 'requirements' of a course.

Yet again — in what way was 'freedom' related to a
demand for standards? Patrick Hughes, when someone
asked the question, during our National Film Theatre event,
'How do you measure standards?' had waved his arm towards the huge transparent ruler that hung down the front
of the cinema screen. And there were the students who
were committed to 'spontaneous' happenings, and insisted
that 'freedom' included the right not to make 'value judgements, man'. But they didn't seem to me to be particularly
'free'; they were very quick to get screwed up if audiences
grew bored or hostile, and they, like any other performers,
wanted to be appreciated, and certainly weren't 'liberated'
by a negative response. On the other hand, by setting
'standards', Jimmy McIlroy *had* extended the 'freedoms'
of the football apprentices — at least in relation to the
demands of their craft. But if the achievement of standards
was an ingredient of freedom — the question was, who
would set the standards? An examining board? A group of
newspaper reviewers? A collection of hand-picked assessors?

It seemed to me, as a teacher, that the only standards
I could honestly apply were my own. Not that my own
standards were individualistic or dilettante: they existed
inside what I considered to be a well-thought-out and coherent intellectual structure, and they had been influenced

by a long tradition which I could trace as far back as
Aristophanes. They were standards that I would apply to
my own work, to the work of any writer I read or to any
play or film I saw — and to the work of any student. To
make allowances, to say, 'well, it's only student work'
always seemed to me to be patronising. I believed that we
should make the highest possible demands, and compare
the work produced with what we considered to be the best
available. The work of the Theatre Group was not as
artistically developed as that of Brecht, or as funny as that
of the Marx Brothers, but *that* was where the comparisons
lay, *those* were the standards we were trying to achieve.

But what was I to do when confronted by students who
didn't share my standards? When, for example, a student
brought me a radio script which aimed at being suitable
for the 'fun' half-hour on Radio Four on Monday mornings, all *Punch* and whimsy, I could either say, 'Well, you
might improve the phrasing there, and that sentence won't
come across very well when it's spoken' — or I could say,
'It's a waste of time asking me what I think about this. I
find the whole thing appalling. But obviously my opinion
isn't shared by the producers of the programmes, or by
the people who listen. You should go and talk to somebody
who likes this kind of stuff.' (Only that, of course, would
be abdicating responsibility for the course . . .)

Again, when a student brought me a heavy 'social
realist' play which he'd submitted for television, and complained that it had been rejected by the company for political reasons, but at the same time asked how he could
improve it so that it might be acceptable — what was I, as
a teacher, supposed to say to him? That I found all such
plays boring, that I thought the form itself was dead, and
that, when a play like that came on, I always tried to find
an old movie on the other channel? And that what he
ought to be doing was trying to find out why routine
television, like *Coronation Street*, worked so well, and
how, if he was so eager to put on a message, he could find
a form which might make it viewable. . . ? These were only
my own opinions, my own standards. I might well be
wrong: but I still felt that if I were honest, as a teacher, all

I could do was recommend him to talk to somebody else.

Yet again, what 'standards' could one apply to the 'happening' boys? There was the student who abandoned one of our theatre games projects after the first day, because he said we were probing his psyche (I thought we were playing games); and then, a few weeks later, was involved in a 'happening' in which he took off a dressing-gown, while a spotlight hovered over him, to reveal that he was naked with a green prick. What was I to say to him afterwards when he asked me how I liked it? 'Very pretty, love.' Or was I to suggest that maybe it was a little bit easy, that a lot of people had done similar 'happenings' before, and that maybe a lot of work and research and thinking was needed before you could make something work? (When I said this I was accused of 'killing enthusiasm'.)

The danger of 'killing enthusiasm' was a very real one. There were so many who gravitated towards the coffee bar. I was, in fact, delighted when students put on events at all — regardless of whether or not they seemed to me to be 'good'. But, all the same, I began to feel like the Red Queen in Alice running faster and faster to stay in the same place. When, for example, a group staged an event in which they forcibly separated members of the audience from their friends, made them sit next to strangers, and then complained that the audience showed hostility ('we just wanted everybody to love each other, man'), it was no use saying, 'But somebody in the Cavern in Liverpool did just that ten years ago, and produced the same effect'. *That* was another time and another place: not to be learned from and built on. To produce instant novelty was more 'creative'.

The problems could, of course, easily have been avoided. We could have announced that we were setting up a 'Brecht laboratory', and, like Grotowski in Poland, have recruited only three or four people a year. But I believed that, given the present oppressive structure of education, it was important to have an area of education where people were free to invent their own programmes, to produce Radio Four whimsy, if that's what they wanted to do, or paint their pricks green. And where else were schoolkids allowed to do what they wanted with the television hardware, even if all they produced in the end was 'I'd like to teach the world to sing'.

At the same time, I was frustrated because it seemed to be increasingly difficult to build on what we'd learned over the previous years. And there were always those students in the coffee bar for whom the course seemed to be doing nothing at all.

The only answer lay in the continual extending of possibilities. I'd believed, in setting up the complementary-studies programme, that we weren't there simply to offer the students what they thought they wanted, but to demonstrate possibilities they'd never even imagined. This had to be a central aim of the full-time course: but it was here that we came up against a problem of simple statistics.

It had been easy to find, out of three hundred students, twelve or fifteen who were willing to commit themselves to the most unexpected projects for one fortnight in the year. The fact that we were offering the programme to so many students meant that we were able to try out any options we could come up with; while the fact that the students were only committing themselves for a fortnight made them willing to take chances too. But when we were trying to plan a programme for only eighteen students, and not for a fortnight, but for three years, it became increasingly difficult to find projects to which enough students would genuinely commit themselves to make the projects worthwhile.

There was always a hard core of students who wanted to involve themselves with Theatre Group work: but, apart from that, the work tended to beome very fragmented. So, one student would stay at home and write television scripts, another would spend his time making a radio tape about mental health, another was working at turning a house into a free school, another was carrying out a very disciplined, but narrow, experiment in film editing. And there were always two or three planning spontaneous happenings.

All these students were committed to work they them-

selves had developed: and one of the aims had been to set
up a course where people *could* develop individual work.
I felt that the work would have made more progress if
they'd developed a more collective approach — but I
equally felt that it wasn't our job to impose collectivity.
People worked fruitfully together when, like the Theatre
Group, they came together out of a common interest —
not because a project was on a time-table. If the students
chose to pursue their interests individually, then that was
their right.

But the real problem was: what about those students
who *hadn't* discovered a commitment, who were sitting
in the coffee bar waiting for something to happen? They
were the ones for whom the course ought to be revealing
new possibilities — but to lay on, for three or four people,
a series of projects, like shots in the dark, in the hope that
something might grab them sometime clearly wasn't much
of a solution.

There were, from time to time, projects that involved
virtually everybody. There was the one, for example, in
which we built the Union Pacific Railway for a week at
the Serpentine Gallery in London. It involved, not only
most of our own students, but people from other departments. So, students from the first year built a structure, like
a three-dimensional jigsaw, that, when put together, became
both a railway and a children's slide. Students from the
textiles department invented and printed witty and elabo-
rately worked fake dollars. Students from the dress section
made clothes for dancing girls in a western bar — and found
themselves playing the parts of the dancing girls. Students
from interior design built a junk city, in the centre of which
was a huge wigwam, which contained, as interior decora-
tion, a three-piece suite, plastic flying ducks and a television set that worked. And the Theatre Group and students
from the course performed in this total context. . . .

It was possible, with projects on this scale, to generate
enthusiasm, collective ideas, commitment. But it was impossible, given our resources, and the way the college was
structured, to organise events of this kind with any regu-
larity. On the other hand, these occasional events – usually

18. *'a structure, like a three-dimensional jig-saw, that . . . became both a* ▶
railway and a children's slide.'

financed from outside the college — did point the way towards possible solutions.

What was clearly needed was a large, comprehensive structure — the educational equivalent of Joan Littlewood's projected 'fun palace' — in which a lot of people were involved, and where a lot of things were continually happening: where, for example, the Theatre Group was pursuing its researches, producing new work, developing new performers; where there was a media research group, extending the ideas into other areas of work; where successful 'professionals' could come and work for particular periods, establishing contacts that could be permanent; where performing artists could invent new events; where news-sheets, poem-posters, comic-books, political pamphlets, T-shirts, mugs with funny faces, art objects of all kinds could be turned out by people working together in a common context; where educational projects, with kids released from school, could rub shoulders with, say, experiments in music; where international footballers without O-levels and university professors sick of their syllabuses could find people to work with.

By the spring of 1973, such a proposition was not impractical. All the elements were there — an open complementary studies structure, a full-time course, a professional theatre group, a scheme for working with school-leavers, an adult education network spread throughout the city, a group of artists in the college who were eager to associate themselves with the work. All that was needed was a way of grouping all these activities together: and we found this in a proposal to form a department of community arts. The proposal was supported by a large majority of the art college staff.

But it was precisely at this moment that the political and administrative contradictions we'd been living with finally caught up with us. In the summer of 1973, the art college was merged with the technical institution across Great Horton Road to form a new Bradford College of Art and Technology. Within a few weeks decisions had been taken which led to the destruction of the work in complementary studies, to the separation of the full-time course from any meaningful context, and to the forcible breaking-up of the team of teachers who had created the work.

Within a few months we were being asked to define our course in terms of 'the intake of the course. . . defining . . . the types of student catered for. . . ; the output — the characteristics and skills of a student who has completed his course and the assumptions about his future career; the programme defined as a process directed at the achievement of objectives operationally defined. . . .'

And a few weeks after that, we were presented with a proposal for a new degree course in design, which was to be submitted to the CNAA — the Council for National Academic Awards. But this was where I'd come in.

Eight years earlier, I'd torn up as impractical a syllabus which included, as a marginal activity, the study of the 'relationship between the artist and his society'. The new syllabus was less modest. Under 'Human Behaviour', along-side 'Experimental Studies in Aesthetics, Year One first term only', and 'Perception, Year One only', the course included 'the study of the relationship between man and his environment'.

Which was somewhat less practical than the syllabus I'd discarded.

Chapter six
Portrait of the educator
as an alienated man

'The world of play is necessarily one of uncertainty and
discovery at every moment, whereas the ambition of the
bureaucrat and the systems-builder is to deal only with
foregone conclusions.'

Marshall McLuhan

'Closely observe the behaviour of these people:
Consider it strange, although familiar,
Hard to explain, although the custom,
Hard to accept, though no exception.
Even the simplest action, apparently simple.
Observe with mistrust. Check whether it is needed
Especially if usual. . . .'

Bertolt Brecht, *The Exception and the Rule*

1

The experiment in alternative education, in this particular
form at least, had been brought to a sudden end. But what
matters in the long run is — what did we learn? What were
we able to demonstrate? Above all, what might be *useful*,
both to ourselves and to other people in future situations?

There are, I believe, three areas in which there are useful
observations to be made. The first relates to the establishment of an alternative *structure* inside an existing education
institution. The second concerns the *learning methods* we
developed through the alternative structure, and their
relationship to what are accepted as the 'normal' learning
methods of the education industry. The third relates to the
creation of an educational vantage point from which it is
possible for individuals and groups to analyse more clearly

the society to which they belong, as a first step towards making necessary changes.

All these areas are closely linked with each other. In this chapter I want to consider some of the positive implications of the work we were able to do.

2

The first point to make about the creation of an alternative structure is that the work actually happened. When I first suggested that education should be about people's wants and desires, and that we needed a structure which would make it possible for people sharing common wants to come together freely and work from common interests, I was told that such a structure would be administratively unworkable. In fact, we demonstrated that a structure involving free choice was comparatively easy to organise (much more easy, for example, than the organisation of a comprehensive school timetable). What was vital was the good-will and active support of the other teachers in the institution. In other words, the workability of an alternative structure depends, not on the limits set by the supposed requirements of bureaucracies, but on the political and educational decisions of those involved. After the Bradford experiment, it remains possible to argue that an alternative structure for liberal education is impractical because those in power can't be persuaded to accept such a structure. It's no longer possible to argue that an alternative structure won't work.

The second point, therefore, relates to how those in power may be persuaded to offer and continue the good-will necessary to the operation. At Bradford we used two methods.

In the first place, we tried to avoid unnecessary confrontations, even when this involved uncomfortable compromises. When, for example, the Principal ordered us to withdraw a pamphlet on *Housing in Bradford*, because it contained a less than liberal quotation by the chairman of the education committee, I agreed to limit the circulation to college students only. (They, of course, made sure that the pamphlet reached anybody who could use it.) Again, when the Principal banned a public performance of a show called *How the Mafia Carved Up Art Education in Bradford*, we cancelled the public showing and performed it in 'private' in our studio — to hundreds of teachers, students and others connected with education. On both occasions we could have staged protests. Instead, we approached authority with good humour and fun, and concentrated on producing more positive work, rather than on striking attitudes.

The second way in which we survived for so long was by using the contradictions of the college situation to identify the institution's interests with our own. I arrived in Bradford at a moment when the college had failed to be awarded the Dip.A.D., and was, therefore, beyond the academic pale. Moreover, large numbers of other art colleges had also been rejected. All were threatened with virtual extinction.

It was urgent for Bradford to find an alternative that would distinguish the college from the rest of these rejects. The radical complementary studies programme offered just such an alternative — particularly when the academically respectable sector of the art college industry encountered its own difficulties at the time of the Hornsey sit-in in 1968. For a time it looked as though the college was going to buy its ticket to academic respectability through the activities of a group of well-published radicals.

In fact, it was only when the institution itself changed its nature by becoming a college of art and technology, and reverted to the aim of achieving status through orthodox degree recognition (not, this time, by means of the Dip. A.D., but at the hands of the CNAA) that the gap between our educational intentions and those of the institution was suddenly thrown into focus, and we were forced, for the moment, into a marginal role.

The set-back demonstrated the limitations of working inside an institution at all. But the alternatives seem to me either to drop out, by setting up free schools and anti-universities, all of which fulfil a useful purpose, but condemn themselves by definition to a marginal place in the community; or to be ready to use the contradictions of a system as it totters into crisis.

Using the contradictions means accepting set-backs — when one set of contradictions is resolved in the wrong way. But each such resolution throws up a new set of contradictions. Which are there also to be used as new situations arise.

3

The second area in which the Bradford experiment demonstrated new possibilities is that of learning method. Nothing is more surprising about the education industry than the relative indifference as to how people learn.

There are, for example, endless discussions — particularly amongst 'progressives' — about *what* people should learn, about curriculum development, the need to introduce 'relevant' subjects (sociology, management, community studies), or the invention of courses geared to specific career prospects. But within the bright new institutions, the method of learning about these 'relevant' topics remains generally unquestioned.

So, in a new comprehensive school, where school-leavers are given a morning's 'community studies', adolescents are encouraged to go to old folks' homes and make cups of tea. But when the 'real' moment of learning comes, they are set to copy out from the *Daily Mirror* stories about old people — just as, if they were more 'academic', they would be copying notes about the French Revolution from a history text-book. They learn as little about old age as their 'academic' counterparts do about Marat.

Again, in the most expensively equipped comprehensive school in the country, a class learns French by using earphones in a language laboratory. They repeat, in unison, the phrases that come over the expensive equipment. They are learning by rote — exactly as *their* counterparts did in the nineteenth century.

What is striking, in fact, about the *practice* of education — as distinct from the organisation and the theorising — is how little has changed in thirty years. My thirteen-year old son is given virtually the same homework that I was given

in the 1940s, and told to do it in the same way: 'Paraphrase
the next sixteen lines in your rough books'. (The sixteen
lines includes one which reads, 'Her sails made pregnant
by the wanton wind.') There's a game I've played with
schoolchildren in all kinds of secondary schools in different parts of the country. It includes forfeits which involve
the players in imitating their teachers. And whenever I play
the game, I recognise the people who taught me thirty
years ago, and the methods they used; the people I taught
with twenty years ago and the methods *they* used; and,
uncomfortably, myself as a schoolmaster.

Examples of the continuity of accepted 'normal' tradi-
tions of learning extend even into the novel areas of educational experiment. So, it's accepted that people demonstrate
what they've learned by writing essays of limited length,
very quickly. Open University students, therefore, are
invited to show their ability as 'historians' by writing on
'How far was the Atlantic Revolution democratic?'; an
international footballer taking a coaching certificate, is
asked to write a forty-minute answer to the question, 'If
you were a manager, how would you put courage into a
timid winger?' ('If either I or the examiners knew the
answer to that,' said Jimmy McIlroy, 'we'd be managing
Real Madrid.')

None of the examples I've given is unusual, or outside
accepted education practice. All of them are essentially
about learning how to make progress in a self-referring
education system which has lost all touch with how people
really learn about things that are useful and enjoyable in
the context of their lived experience.

It was with an awareness of the unreality of the learning
situation I found myself in at Bradford that I began to
question not only what I was doing but how I was doing it.
There I was, in a lecture room, with sixty students who
happened to be grouped together because they were label-
led 'Pre-Diploma', and with whom I was analysing the opening sequence of a Jean Renoir film because 'film' was my
'subject', and was supposed to be 'relevant' to art students.
Not more than a handful of those students would ever find
a practical use for what we were doing. And those who did

would learn about Renoir in quite a different context from
one in which we were all locked together because 'they' —
the education industry — ordered it so.

Faced with this unreal learning situation, a group of us
tried to create alternative situations in which learning became part of a concrete, physical experience. So: we played children's games. And, in playing them, we created
situations that were 'real', in the simplest sense. If the aim
was to catch a ball, and you dropped it, you lost the game.
In playing the games, we discovered that the game situations opened up possibilities of communication on a totally
different level from that of the 'discussion'. People who
spoke up in discussions were usually playing the 'getting
on in education' game: that is, they were talking because
what they had to say would benefit them in some academic
assessment. But people who, in team games, talked to the
rest of the team about what the next move should be, were
doing so because they wanted to win that game, there and
then. In this kind of situation, people became invokved for
an immediate purpose. Experiences became memorable,
not because a teacher said, 'this is important: commit it to
your memory', but because the experiences themselves
were enjoyable. Students who had been written off as 'non-
verbal' became articulate, because they were operating
inside a structure they could handle. Students who were
thought of an 'non-intellectual' offered thought-out solutions of which I would have been incapable. The games
were connected with practical learning processes.

Then we went on to the handling of complex intellectual
ideas through games situations. When we staged a Russian
Revolution in the streets, practical problems were involved.
We had to make and distribute posters. But what *ideas*
were the posters trying to communicate. Mayakovsky
became, not a remote name in art history, but someone
whose ideas, if we could understand them, and whose
example, if we could follow and adapt it, became a real
element in a practical situation. We had to study the map
of what happened in St Petersburg — and therefore the
events which made the map — because we were trying to
reproduce that map on a map of Bradford. We had to in-

vent rules that were related to the original historical events, and therefore to study those events — but the rules had to work in Forster Square Station and Manningham Lane. The fact that the event took place at all demonstrated the practicality of the learning processes involved.

Later, we taught each other how to do quadratic equations by moving people around in a room; we came to grips with the latest theories about quasars by drawing lines on a balloon; we delved into the history of the cold war by setting up a western gun-fight. At every point, we tried to make knowledge concrete. And in doing so we acquired practical skills. When the Theatre Group prepared public entertainments, they had to learn how to deliver lines and make gestures in such a way as to make audiences laugh. They didn't learn 'speech' and 'movement', as subjects: they learned how to solve problems that were immediate and real. And the success of their learning was tested in real situations, in front of people who had come to be entertained, and not a group of select examiners.

And when the examiners did come to assess students' work, and one of them asked, 'But what have they *learnt?*', the students, listening through a tape-recorder in the next room, roared with laughter. What one of them had learnt was how to bug his own assessment.

The learning methods we discovered and evolved were both concrete and practical. But the irony was that in the context of what is accepted as 'normal' in the education industry, they were highly impractical.

The point was demonstrated for us by the international footballer, Jimmy McIlroy, who has worked with us on a number of projects. He is as intelligent and articulate as he is skilled: but when, at the end of his career, he offered himself as a teacher of football skills to the education authority of the town where he had been a football hero, he was asked, 'How many O-levels do you have?' He had none: and so there was no job for him. Whereas I, as a teacher of French with an Oxford degree and an education diploma, and very little skill with a football, was recognised as being qualified to teach 'games'. McIlroy's practical skills were not only *seen* as impractical. They were *made* impractical by the decree of what Illich calls 'the self-certifying professional elite', who only recognise as practical those skills (such as the passing of examinations) which they themselves have found to be useful.

In the same way the administration of the new College of Art and Technology could only see the work we were doing as 'impractical', because it was not related to the practical aims of the new institution — the acquiring of CNAA degrees. The fact that, in helping us evolve new, concrete methods of learning, 'non-academic' students had produced work of the highest academic quality, was less 'real' than the fact that we were unable to describe our work in terms of 'Input', 'Output' and pre-conceived annual objectives.

But at this point it becomes necessary to examine the relationship of an industry which can declare 'unreal' the skills of a McIlroy, or 'impractical' an educational method based on practicalities, to the whole social reality of which that industry is a part. And it is here that the work we developed at Bradford offers something more than an alternative way of acquiring socially acceptable skills. It provides a way of looking at a society that is itself in many ways 'unreal', and of which the unreality of the education industry is no more than a reflection.

4

The society to which we all belong is one which is based on such grotesque fantasies that it can only be maintained by a system of perpetual mystification. To select only one example: the defence of that society, which locks up vast financial resources that are related to the mystifying phrases such as 'balance of payments deficit', 'cash flow', depends, quite simply, on the society's stated willingness to kill, by the use of Polaris, enough people to make Auschwitz an amateur exercise in massacre, in order to gain political ends. That the threat is not an idle one is demonstrated by our willingness to use, and justify, similar techniques in the Second World War: Dresden, Hiroshima and Nagasaki are concrete statements to the effect that we believe in massacre when it advances our own cause. Yet when the IRA (a subversive group that would have been admired had it been called the Maquis, and operated against the German army instead of the British) borrows, on a tiny scale, this 'realistic' philosophy, all the abstract moralities are suddenly released. What is realistic policy, when applied to international affairs, becomes barbaric terrorism, when it happens in Guildford or Birmingham. And highly civilised men, who defend the burning alive of children in Dresden, demand the return of hanging to deal with the IRA monsters.

Such a schizophrenic approach to reality can only be maintained by a systematic diminution of social awareness. George Orwell pointed to such a diminution as long ago as 1946, in an essay called *Politics and the English Language*. He wrote:

> In our time, political speech and writings are largely the defence of the indefensible. . . . Defenceless villages are bombarded from the air, the inhabitants driven out into the countryside, the cattle machine-gunned: this is called *pacification*. Millions of peasants are robbed of their farms and sent trudging along the roads with no more than they can carry: this is called *transfer of population* or *rectification of frontiers*. People are imprisoned for years without trial or shot in the back of the neck or sent to die of scurvy in Arctic lumber camps: this is called *elimination of unreliable elements*.

Orwell didn't live to hear successive US administrations describe as 'defending the Four Freedoms' a process involving the killing, maiming or rendering homeless of several million Asian peasants. But he did point towards a process by which, in whole areas of our social experience, the gap between awareness and reality threatened to turn into a fixed gulf.

The gap springs, not so much from a lack of knowledge — people in our society know, in a superficial and cliched way, far more about what's going on in the world than any other society has ever known — as from a failure of the

imagination. Paradoxically, the proliferation on a certain
level of a particular kind of knowledge, reflecting a picture
of the world acceptable to the controlling élite, (in the
form, for example, of newsreels of concentration camps,
starving refugees, public executions, or, for that matter, of
statistics about inflation, or the population explosion) leads
to a slackening of the imaginative grip. It's like the effects
of pornography — the kicks lessen with familiarity. Moreover, both newsreels and statistics come across with a
sense of inevitability. Napalmed children are sad: still,
that's life, and we can't do anything about it, any more
than we can do anything about the price of petrol.

In such a situation, what is needed is not yet more of
this kind of controlled knowledge, but the ability to put
what is known to social use. This demands in the first place,
an act of the imagination. When you're trapped inside a
room, in which all the windows are distorting mirrors, it's
no good looking in the mirror and describing more and
more of what you see. You've got to make some kind of
imaginative leap, to get yourself out of the closed room, to
be able to look at your situation from some kind of
distance.

It was this need that drove Kurt Vonnegut, when he
wanted to describe the reality of his own experience of
Dresden, to write a piece of science fiction and invent a
fantasy world called Tralfamadore. And it was the same
need that drove us away from 'documentary' and 'the
theatre of fact' and into an area of metaphor and play.

When we pretended that Bradford was St Petersburg, or
that we were stars in a western playing at being Kennedy,
or an army being led by Wilson to Dunkirk; or when we
told the story of Hitler in the form of a Passion Play, we
weren't escaping into fantasy. We were trying to illuminate
that world. Commenting on *John Ford's Cuban Missile
Crisis*, Barnet K. Kellman wrote, in *Time Out:*

> It does nothing less than counteract the anesthesia of
> twenty-odd years of crisis politics on television with
> a healthy dose of laughing gas. It reawakens us to the
> *pain and reality of our situation. . . .*

This was certainly our intention, not because we wanted to indulge ourselves in the luxury of pain, but because we saw the imaginative reawakening as a necessary first step towards regaining control of that situation.

And in this sense the political content of the Theatre Group's work rose directly out of the educational situation in which the work had been created. There was a direct connection between my first imaginative awareness of the impracticality of standing in a lecture room analysing a Renoir film, and our group awareness of the incredibility of a man whose 'most solemn feelings concerned the killing of children' — but who was prepared to burn the lot alive rather than lose political face.

The alternative education structure at Bradford had been created by an act of the imagination. Stepping outside the self-referring world of accepted forms of education, we'd asked ourselves, 'What can we invent that will *work*?' We'd dreamed up a practical situation and then acted to bring it into being. And the existence of that situation had made possible more acts of imagination; which in turn gave us weapons with which to assault the mystifications of a society intent on hiding its true identity behind a curtain of jargon.

And this, to me, is what is of lasting importance about our work at Bradford: that we created forms and ways of working that enabled us to understand, cut down to size, and, in some cases, destroy the mystifications that surrounded us. Mystifications in all shapes and sizes.

When we looked at films, in the National Film Theatre, through the eyes of alien intelligences, we were mocking the the mystification that films can only be truly understood by 'experts'. When we presented, in the Wilson show, an agit-prop 'Play within a Play' demonstrating the workings of foreign aid, we were both exposing the mystifications of television economics, and enjoying ourselves at the expense of the solemnities of some agit-prop theatre. When we built a sculpture, in the Serpentine Gallery, that turned

19. *'When we presented, in the Wilson show, an agit-prop "Play within a Play", demonstrating the workings of foreign aid, we were both exposing the mystifications of television economics, and enjoying ourselves at the expense of the solemnities of some agit-prop theatre*

itself into an adventure playground for shouting kids, and when we turned one wing of the gallery into a pub that was open all afternoon, with honky-tonk piano and all, we were demolishing the mystification that makes art galleries feel like churches. When we put the parable of the talents into the mouth of Hitler, we were not only satirising his Messiah-like behaviour, but also the mystification that reads into the parable a meaning that isn't there.

And when we made a Mafia play about the technical college merger, we used exactly the same methods we had used on Churchill, Kennedy, Wilson and Hitler to demystify the college situation: and the fact that the script was made up in part from confidential memoranda and minutes, which I'd dumped on the studio floor, considerably de-mystified what was going on behind the closed doors in the circle of the powerful.

And this is what matters in the end about the work in Bradford: not that, as a result of decisions taken by sections of the 'self-certifying professional élite' remote from our working situation, that work never realised its full possibilities; but that the methods we invented to demonstrate, through play, fun and imagination, that élite's ultimate irrelevance are there, waiting to be used, by anybody, anywhere.

And that the process of inventing those methods was very enjoyable. As Brecht puts it: 'Nothing needs less justification than pleasure.'

Appendix One

A number of teachers have asked me for lists or descriptions of games that have proved to be useful in teaching situations. I believe that it's important for individual teachers to find their own games, and their own uses for them. Indeed, it's important to leave the 'use' as wide open as possible: if a teacher knows, or thinks he knows, precisely what he hopes to develop from a game, he's liable to try and force the end result, and, in doing so, limit the actual possibilities. For each new learning situation, each different group throws up its own possibilities. For the game to be really useful, the teacher himself has to learn from those possibilities. An adult education tutor, a sociologist, recently told me that she'd only consider using games (which she called 'role-playing exercises') with groups to 'drive home' points she'd already 'made clear' in other ways. None of the games described here is intended to be used as a way of 'driving home' points of which the teacher already considers himself to be certain. They are intended to create concrete situations in which everybody, including the teacher, can learn.

If the situation is genuinely open, and allowed to develop at its own speed and in its own way, the teacher will find the group suggesting new games, new variations, new ways of developing what is happening. All the same — everybody has to start somewhere. I started with a book of games for boy scouts, which I strongly recommend.

With the above reservations in mind, here are a few of the games I personally have found most useful, and some descriptions of the ways they have sometimes developed.

1. Ball Games

Particularly useful for releasing energy, for destroying self-consciousness and inhibitions about 'performance', for developing physical coordination in groups, and also for developing concentration.

a)   A lively game is for everybody to form a circle, with one person in the middle. The aim is for people in the circle to throw the ball so as to hit the one in the middle below the knee. The one in the middle has to avoid the ball. It's possible to build up skills in passing the ball quickly around and across the circle, building up a sense of teamwork, instead of individual brute force. The one who succeeds in hitting, with the ball, the person in the middle, takes his place. At a later stage, the one in the middle may be asked to be making a speech, telling a joke, singing a song, reciting a poem etc., while still trying to avoid the ball. Another variation is for the first one in the middle to begin telling a story, which has to be continued by whoever takes his place — so that gradually a continual and collective story is built up by people who are, at the same time, skipping to avoid being hit by the ball. . . .

b)   Another energy-releasing game: people form a circle, turn right, then march round in the circle while passing a ball from one to another. Each person throws the ball over his head to the person behind. The aim is not to drop the ball. To add to the enjoyment, the group may sing while marching. It's fairly easy to pass the ball round while marching, so after a time, somebody should give the order to run. After that, it becomes more difficult. A chair is then placed in the centre, and anybody who drops the ball has to stand on the chair, make a speech, tell a joke, recite, sing etc., until the next person who drops the ball replaces him on the chair. . . . Variations to this are to have several objects e.g. a milk bottle, a handbag, a box of matches, a knotted scarf — also being passed round the circle at the same time as the ball. Each time one is dropped, the victim has to stand on the chair in the middle and 'perform' . . . . In other variations, specific problems can be set. At what speed does the circle have to move so that the ball is always thrown in the same place — in other words so that it simply goes up and down in the air, without moving round the circle? (We used this exercise for a scene in *Quasar* in which the ball became a planet whose constant orbit was studied by an astronomer.)

c)   A good concentration game is simply for people to stand in a circle and throw the ball at random to each other. Anybody who drops the ball leaves the game, so that, in the end, it's a battle of concentration between three and then two people. Or, two objects — a ball and, say, a handbag — can be thrown round the circle: each thrower throws the objects to the person standing next but one on his left: it works best if there are an odd number of people in the circle. As the group becomes more skilled, more objects may be added, until a whole set of different objects with different textures are going round at the same speed. The players may then be invited to tell a story as the objects are going round: or to rehearse a simple script.

2. Rough and Tumble Games

These are useful for releasing energy — and for making people less inhibited about physical contact.

a)   BRITISH BULLDOG: a strong, powerful person is invited to stand in the middle of the room. The rest of the group line up along one wall. At a given signal, the group tries to rush across the room to the opposite wall. The one in the centre tries to catch them. In order to catch anybody, he has to lift the victim completely off the ground: the person who has been caught now joins the catcher in the middle of the room. The game goes on until all except one have been caught. The one who has not been caught now becomes the 'bulldog' in the middle, the rest line up along one wall, and the game begins again. The only other rules are that players only try to cross the room each time a referee gives a signal: and that once a player has crossed, and is touching the opposite wall, he can't re-cross until the next signal is given. He is, however, allowed to help to pull in people who are struggling to escape from the 'bulldog', by reaching out one hand, as long as the other hand remains touching the wall. The game works best with mixed groups of boy and girl students. Players should be encouraged to play with enthusiasm — that is, to struggle against being lifted from the ground. (For an excellent variation, see 'Blindfold Games' below.)

b)   CHALK RUGBY: a very simple game. Two chairs are placed, one at each end of the room. The group is divided into two equal teams. The referee starts the game by throwing a piece of chalk into the air. Goals are scored by making a cross with a piece of chalk on the opponents' chair. There are no other rules.

c)   BREAK THE CIRCLE: a circle is formed, with all the players holding hands. One person is trapped inside the circle, another is shut out. The one outside is trying to get in, the one inside is trying to get out. Those who form the circle are trying to prevent this, and also trying to prevent the circle from ever being broken.

d)   HYDE PARK CORNER: four chairs are placed in a line at one end of the room. Four players stand, one on each chair, and make speeches, all at the same time, about anything they like. The aim of each player is to speak louder and longer than any of the others. Below them, keeping guard, are a number of 'policemen', there to ensure 'free speech'. (The number of policemen depends on the number of people playing: there need to be enough to make some pretence of 'keeping order' but not so many that their task is easy.) If there are a lot of players, some may be spectators, listening to the speeches. Suddenly, a strange procession enters. They are marching in an orderly file and singing, very loudly, some piece of nonsense, a nursery rhyme, for example — 'Baa, baa, black sheep'. . . . They sing it repeatedly, over and over again, as loudly as possible, trying to drown the speakers on the chairs. They stand in front of the speakers until the police decide to order them to move on. The 'demonstrators' are not willing to move on: so the police have to move them. The 'demonstrators' must remain strictly non-violent: they may link arms, sit, cling to the chairs, go limp, but they must not fight back. If individual demonstrators are arrested and dragged off by the police, they have the right to escape, as soon as possible, and re-join the game. The game goes on until everybody has had enough.

3. Games of Tag

The variations and uses are endless. 'How', an HMI once asked me, 'would you show anarchy turning into order?' I set up a game in which one person was trying to tag the others: the first person he tags joins hands with him, and together they try and tag another, who then also join hands; and then the three of them tag another, so that there are four of them holding hands and trying to tag, and so on. . . . Eventually, all except one are holding hands in a line and trying to tag the one who is left. . . . This particular game began with everybody rushing madly around the room, and ended, a minute or so later, with them all standing in a circle holding hands. Anarchy to order. . . .

The two most useful tag games, I've found, are:

a)   CHINESE LAMP-POSTS: one person is trying to tag the rest. When a person is tagged he/she has to stand with his/her legs wide open, and can be liberated by one of the other non-tagged players crawling between his/her legs. When a person has been caught three times, he/she drops out. The game ends when either everybody has been caught three times, or there is nobody free to do the 'liberating'. (For an interesting variation of this, see 'Blindfold Games'.)

b)   THE PENNY GAME: one person is trying to tag the rest. But a penny (or some other easily distinguishable coin) is handed to the rest of the group. A person can only actually be caught if he is holding the penny. The aim of the 'tagger', therefore, is to tag the person he thinks has the penny, the aim of the group is to pass the penny from one to another so that the 'tagger' never finds it and nobody is ever caught. This is a good energy-releasing game when played while running, but if it is slowed to a walk it becomes something else again. We usually have the rule that nobody is allowed to run, that people must walk with their hands behind their backs, passing the coin surreptitiously from one to the other. When anybody is touched by the 'tagger', he/she must stop and show both hands. The game has proved capable of considerable development. It's good for two or three always to drop out and watch, to try and observe for themselves where the coin is travelling, to see whether people behave differently when they are carrying the coin. As the group becomes more skilful, people begin to pretend to have the coin when they don't have it, take risks, succeed in passing the coin in front of the 'tagger's' nose. Spectators can observe whether players succeed *accurately* in their imitations of people carrying the coin. . . pretending to have it when they don't. Another variation is for the players to be instructed always to *show* the coin to the spectators, while not allowing the 'tagger' to see it. It's possible, with a group who have become really skilled, to build up 'street scenes' while playing this game: a policeman, for example, is quietly searching people for 'pot'; each player in the game has to become a person in a street, a newspaper-seller, a woman with a pram, two may become a courting couple, and all the time the 'policeman' is touching people, asking them to show their hands — and the coin is being passed round. (This variation really does demand a lot of skill.) In other variations, players may be asked to take on particular movements — limping, hopping, dragging one foot — and to keep to these while playing the game. One of the most interesting variations we developed involved the use of masks (see the section on the production of *Ars Longa, Vita Brevis*).

4. Blindfold Games

These can be extremely productive. They are particularly helpful for students who are not particularly verbal, and who are able to demonstrate qualities of intelligence that are not related to a discussion situation.

The simplest (the one from which we started *Performance*) consists of two people, A and B, wearing blindfolds. The rest of the group forms a square around them, and somewhere in the playing area, an agreed object (e.g. a slipper) is placed. A is looking for the slipper; B is looking for A. If B touches A the game is over: similarly, if A finds the slipper, the game is over. The game can be even more effectively played with four people, two As and two Bs. When a B catches an A, A's mask is removed, and the A drops out of the game. It's important that the spectators should be completely still and silent, since much of the tension springs from the sounds that are made in the silence. (For a variation on this game, see the account of *Performance*.)

Another interesting blindfold game is a development of the tag game, *Chinese Lamp-posts*. All the players have blindfolds. One player (the 'tagger') is given an object (e.g. a slipper). When the 'tagger' catches anybody he/she touches him/her with the slipper, in such a way that the person knows he/she has been caught. The person who has been caught then stands with his/her legs open, waiting to be liberated (i.e for another player to crawl between his/her legs.) To attract attention, the person who has been caught is allowed to make any sound (e.g. clapping, clucking like a hen, mooing etc.), but not to utter words. When a person has been caught three times, he/she drops out; when all are caught the game ends. This makes for a very interesting game, both for players and spectators. Again — it's important that the spectators should remain silent.

A version of *British Bulldog* can be played blindfold. There is a 'bulldog', a killer, in the middle of the room, with, say, a slipper. When players are touched by the slipper, as they try to cross the room, they know they are killed, and must lie down. There is, however, also a 'resurrector', with, for example, a milk bottle: so that when the dead bodies are touched by the milk bottle, they know they have been resurrected. Moreover, anybody, except the killer, has the right to use the milk-bottle. So: if the original 'resurrector' is 'killed', someone else has the right to find the milk bottle, and use it to resurrect the dead. This means that all the players are constantly groping around the room, looking for the milk-bottle — while the killer, with the slipper, is looking for everybody else. We once played this game in a totally blacked-out room, without blindfolds. The room was so completely blacked-out that not a chink of light was visible. After three hours, nobody knew any longer the shape of the room. It was a most concentrated and mind-blowing experience.

There's another entertaining blindfold game — for knockabout fun — in which two players are given blindfolds, put in corners of the room, and handed rolled-up newspapers. The aim of each player is to advance towards the opponent and hit him with the paper. A variation is to have four players, one in each corner of the room.

Another entertaining game — both with and without blindfolds — takes the form of a relay race. There are two equal teams, who line up behind a leader. The leader stands with his/her legs apart, and No. 1 in each team has to crawl between the leader's legs, run and touch the opposite wall, and come back and collect No. 2. Nos 1 and 2, holding hands, then repeat the process and come back and collect No. 3. Eventually, there are two long chains of people trying to crawl, holding hands, through the leader's legs, run and touch the opposite wall and return. If the chain breaks, or the leader loses balance, the move has to start again.

When the game is played blindfold, two players, making distinctive sounds, stand by the opposite wall to guide the rival teams. The leaders, with their legs open, have the right to make the same sounds.

A more complex blindfold game is one used with Peter Brook in *US*. A structure is built which enables the players to cross the room without touching the floor. Three 'victims' are placed at one end of the structure, each 'victim' being allowed to make a distinctive sound. Three 'helpers' are then introduced to search for the 'victims' —one for each 'victim'. Both 'victims' and 'helpers' are wearing blindfolds: and none of the players must touch the floor. The spectators are allowed to make sounds to distract the players: we found it most effective when there was a conductor, who signalled periods of silence, followed by periods of bedlam.

There are a great many more variations of blindfold games. They are usually much enjoyed, both by players and spectators; and teachers and students should try and invent their own variations.

5. The Scissors Game

This is a daft game, but very useful because players who are 'non-academic' often spot it very quickly, whereas lecturers on 'lateral thinking' can be left stranded. Everybody sits in a circle. Somebody with a pair of scissors announces that he's going to pass on the scissors either 'crossed' or 'uncrossed'. He then does a complicated routine with the scissors and announces 'They're crossed'. He asks the person to his left to pass on the scissors, to the person to *his* left, either 'crossed' or 'uncrossed'. The point is that the crossing and un-crossing has nothing to do with the scissors, but with legs: you pass the scissors on with your legs either crossed or uncrossed. The game is very entertaining, if it's not carried too far: I've even used it to demonstrate Brechtian theatre: are you merely listening to the words, or looking at the total image?

6. Interaction Game

This, again, is particularly good for demonstrating that 'intelligence' is not necessarily connected with verbal skills. It's played by two people. The first goes out of the room, and the second then tells the spectators, 'I'm going to make the other player do a particular action (or speak a particular phrase)'; e.g. touch a wall, sit on a chair, open a window, light a cigarette, say 'Thank you'. The first player then leaves the room and the second player then tells the spectators what he/she is going to make the first player do/say. The development of the game depends very much on the willingness of the players to explore possibilities: it can reach stalemate if neither will do or say anything! For this reason, it's as well to put a time-limit, say ten minutes. The player wins who forces (not physically, but through cunning) the opponent to carry out the pre-declared action, or speak the pre-declared phrase.

7. Simon Says

A very simple game, which quickens physical response. One person gives instructions to the rest: 'Simon says touch your toes'; 'Simon says hop on your right foot.' Players have to obey Simon's instructions: but if Simon doesn't say it, if, for example, the leader says simply, 'Touch your toes', then you mustn't obey. Players who make mistakes drop out.

8. Grandmother's Footsteps

One player stands facing the wall at the end of a long room. The rest try and creep up and touch him. He turns round at unexpected intervals. If he sees people moving, he sends them back to start again. When he is eventually touched, he turns and chases everybody. The person he catches is the one who next faces the wall. In one of the most interesting variations of this game, we tied objects, which made noises, to the players — chains that dragged, brushes that swished, even desks. . . . The sense was of grotesque noisily playing what was supposed to be a silent children's game. A very useful variation was to make the person facing the wall a schoolteacher, writing on a blackboard. The rest sat around in a semi-circle. While the teacher wrote on the blackboard, the rest tried to change chairs

with each other. If the 'teacher' caught anybody moving, that person
had to become the teacher and continue the lesson. It's a good game
to play with schoolchildren: you ask them, if they're caught, to
imitate a teacher they know. The results are very revealing.

9. The Holy Dido

This game is either enjoyed so much that people play it for hours —
or detested. The players sit in a circle. There is a President, who gives
them numbers. The President holds an object, e.g. a slipper, which
is declared to be 'the Holy Dido'. He places the object at his feet,
and announces, 'The court is in session.' While the court is in session,
all the members must sit with their arms folded and their feet
crossed. They must also behave with complete gravity, i.e. they must
not smile or laugh.

The object, the sole object, of the members of the court is to
accuse their fellow members of breaking the rules. There is a ritual
for this. If a member wishes to accuse another member of uncros-
sing arms or legs, or, more likely, of grinning, he raises his hand. The
President of the court then says, 'Rise no. so-and-so.' No. so-and-so
says, 'Permission to speak?', and the President says, 'Take the Holy
Dido.' No. so-and-so then takes the Holy Dido and says, 'I accuse
No. 3 of scratching his ear' — or whatever. The President can then
order punishment — strokes with the Holy Dido on either the 'upper
deck' (the hand) or the 'lower deck' (the behind). The punishment
must be delivered with the utmost gravity. The game has to be
played very seriously; and we normally agree that if the President of
the Court blatantly breaks the rules (e.g. laughs) he hands over his
position, and the Holy Dido, to another player. The game was used
by Clive Barker, of Joan Littlewood's Theatre Workshop, as a way
of staging a court scene from Cervantes. We've found it entertaining in its own right. This game also is capable of variations, which
enterprising players may discover for themselves.

The games I've described are just a few of the many we've enjoyed
playing. People should, above all, try and discover — and develop —
their own games. Quite apart from the ideas which may develop
from them, they are enjoyable for their own sake: and, as Brecht
says, 'Nothing needs less justification than pleasure' — particularly
in the world of education.

10. Improvisations

In addition to the games, there are a number of game/improvisations
which I've found particularly useful. Here are three:
a) a man comes back to his flat one night and discovers a completely
strange girl watching his television. The girl insists that the flat is
hers. How does the relationship develop?

b) A girl telephones her parents, who have told her to be in by eleven, to explain that she's staying out for the night. An extension of this is: a girl arrives home very late, to find her father sitting in a chair waiting for her. If she can talk her way past him into the bedroom, she's won the game. (An entertaining variation of this is for the father to pretend he's John Wayne, and for the girl to play Marilyn Monroe.)
c) A middle-class housewife is telephoning her hairdresser, when a policeman knocks at the door. The policeman orders her to come to the police-station, but is not at liberty to explain why. He's only obeying orders. The game is won/lost either when she gets rid of him, or he persuades her to come with him. (This too is capable of endless variation.)

Improvisations often work best when a 'play' element is introduced — for example when the performers are asked to pretend to be famous film-stars. This produces an element of distance — and, paradoxically, allows the real elements in the situation to emerge much more clearly.

I used to be told that only people of certain ages would play. I don't any longer accept this: but clearly any teacher who wants to play games with pupils or students has to establish first the right relationship. And to be willing to play himself/herself. And to be willing to lose. . . .

Appendix Two

A lot of teachers have said to me that the complementary studies programme must have been difficult to organise. In fact, it was a good deal more simple than, for example, the normal comprehensive school timetable.

Every year, all the members of the team used to meet during the summer and put forward ideas for the next year's programme. Sometimes the ideas were what they themselves had thought of and wanted to do; sometimes they were ideas suggested by students. The members of the team also suggested people they had met, or heard of, during the previous year, who might like to come and do projects. One of us approached these people, asking 'If you were completely free to do what you liked with a group of students for a fortnight, what would you want to do?'

In this way we would put a year's programme together, from our ideas, from the ideas of students, and from the ideas of people who were available, and we would offer this programme to all the students in college. The programme would be ready before the beginning of term, and every student would be handed a programme on enrolment. Attached to the programme was a slip, for student choices. Students were asked to offer their first, second and third choices, and it was also made clear that if none of the projects appealed to a particular student, that student would have the right to come and see us and discuss what form his complementary studies might take. Students were also asked to talk with their own departmental students, and find out if there were any periods of the year at which it would be difficult for them to take part in a project.

The students were given about three weeks to make their choices: and during these three weeks, the complementary studies staff were available in the departments to talk to tutors and students about the programme. When all the students choices were in, the complementary studies staff went through the choices allocating students to particular projects. Students were also informed at this stage that if they objected to the allocation, they were free to discuss the question with the staff. Lists of all the projects and the students allocated to them were then sent out to all departments, so that students and tutors could know when the students would be missing from the departments, and complementary studies staff could know precisely what students were on which project.

The following is an example of the information that was sent out to students and staff:

Regional College of Art, Bradford
COMPLEMENTARY STUDIES: 1967 — 1968
. . . .

The complementary studies work this year has once again been built around a programme of projects. Each project will last for two weeks, and will be followed up by ten evening seminars.

Every full-time student in college will be required to undertake *one* fortnightly project during the year, together with the follow-up seminars.

Students have the right, in consultation with their tutors, to choose which project they will undertake. A varied programme has been prepared to cover as many interests as possible.

Study this programme carefully to see which projects appeal to you. Then fill in the attached form, suggesting THREE projects in order of preference. When you have completed the form, return it to your section head.

Note: some projects will probably turn out to be more heavily booked than others. There is a strict limit to the numbers we can take on any one project. If you wish to be accepted for your first choice, make sure your form is returned promptly.

. . . .

Autumn Term

P1   October 2nd — 13th
'ALL YOU NEED IS LOVE' — the Beatles
Tutor: Albert Hunt

One of the main topics of all popular entertainment — comics, films, songs — is love. Love at first sight, love eternal, love unrequited. . . .
What picture of love do we get from the pops? Has this picture changed at all in the last few years? And what is the connection between love in the pops and what happens in everyday life?
In this project, we shall begin by examining some popular films, songs and comics. We shall then talk to people of all ages, making tape recordings and comparing the results with the pop ideas. We shall discuss the attitudes of other societies (e.g. South Sea Islands) towards love. And we shall end by trying to make our own comment on the subject — through sound, visuals, writing and acting.

P2   October 9th — 20th
PREPARING AN EVENT
Tutor: Stephen Brook

This project is particularly intended for students interested in learning how to organise activities, either through the Students' Union or other groups. It is vital for anyone wishing to work on the Students' Union Committee, in any capacity.
Students will be responsible, under Stephen Brook, for organising a college event. They will learn how to plan a programme, to contact artists, to handle finances and to deal with publicity.
The event will take place shortly after the end of the project.
Stephen Brook was responsible for organising the highly successful 4 July celebration last term.

P3   October 23rd — November 3rd
SPARE THE ROD
Tutor: Graham Owens

This summer, an approved school was closed after disclosures about caning. What exactly happens in schools for young offenders? How does authority cope with social rebels? What attitudes to education shape these institutions? And how do these attitudes affect the rest of us?

In this project, we shall visit a number of approved schools and Borstals, talk to young people who have been inside them, and look at a school that believes in freedom.

Graham Owens is a Senior Lecturer at the Margaret McMillan College of Education.

P4   October 23rd — November 3rd
ST PETERSBURG 1917 / BRADFORD 1967: an October Carnival
Tutors: John and Margaretta Arden

This October is the 50th anniversary of the Russian Revolution, an event which, in a few days, changed the course of world history.

During this project, we shall be studying the events of the October Revolution, looking at films, listening to expert speakers, with a view to re-creating some of those events, in dramatic form, in the streets of Bradford. We shall turn Bradford into St Petersburg, making our own maps and moving into strategic parts of the city. Lenin will arrive in a train from Liverpool; we shall produce our own newsheets; and it is hoped to film some of the main activities.

We shall need a large number of students to take part in this adventure; not just those who are already interested in political history, but any who would like the opportunity of helping to create a unique dramatic event. We shall want people to make banners and puppets, to write and film, and to play some of the leading historical roles. Anyone with ideas will be welcomed.

John Arden is one of our leading playwrights: Margaretta Arden is a professional actress, and has also collaborated in the writing of many of her husband's plays. Wherever they have gone, things have happened: last term, for example, they were at New York University, where they produced together an eight hour war carnival.

If you want to take part — apply early.

This could be the happening of the year.

P5   November 6th — 17th
POP, JAZZ & FOLK
Tutors: Stephen Brook and John Gascoigne

All over the district, popular music of all kinds is flourishing. There are jazz clubs, beat clubs, folk clubs, all with their own following and their own performers.

What kind of people belong to these clubs? What about the performers? Who are they? Do they make much money? And

how are they organised? What makes some people prefer one
sort of music to another?

In this project, we shall try to find out as much as possible
about the local pop scene and about the music. At the end of
the project we shall try and present an entertainment — of
pop, jazz and folk.

P6   November 27th — December 8th
      THEATRE PROJECT
      Tutors: Geoffrey Reeves and Albert Hunt

For anyone interested in making theatre that is alive. There
will be games, improvisations and experiments, leading towards
work on a script which we as a group will create.

Geoffrey Reeves is a professional director, rapidly acquiring
an international reputation. He is at present in Stockholm,
directing a Swedish version of US.

Spring Term

P7   January 15th — 26th
      MAKING A MAGAZINE
      Tutor: Stephen Brook

This project is for anyone interested in helping to design and
produce a college magazine. We do not intend that this should
be a conventional magazine. Both the form and content will,
we hope, be original — but that depends largely on the people
taking part.

A particular aim will be to provide encouragement to students who want to write. All kinds of writing will be welcomed.

P8   January 29th — February 9th
      THE DESTRUCTION OF DRESDEN: AN INVESTIGATION
      Tutor: Albert Hunt

On the night of the 13-14 February, 1945, the city of Dresden
was destroyed in the heaviest air raids in history, and 145,000
people were killed.

A few months later, the war ended and the Nazi leaders
were put on trial at Nuremberg. Years after the end of the
Nuremberg trials, Adolf Eichmann was kidnapped and tried at
Jerusalem for his part in exterminating millions of Jews.

If the Nazis had won the war, would they themselves have
staged war crimes trials? What if they had tried those who
planned and carried out the destruction of Dresden? What
would the defence have been, and how would it have differed
from the defence of Eichmann and the rest?

In this project, we shall play out parts of the Nuremberg
and Eichmann trials, shall read Peter Weiss's play *The Investi-*

gation, and shall then try and stage our own trial of Dresden.
It is hoped that we shall be able to present this on the anniversary of Dresden, and that a number of law experts will be
taking part.

P9   February 12th — February 23rd
     THE JUNK TRADE
     Tutor: John Gascoigne

Junk is in fashion. People who want to be with it haunt junk
shops — see Antonioni's film about swinging London, *Blow Up*.
     But junk is also a business, and in the Bradford area there
are dozens of people who make a living selling junk. Who are
these people? How did they get into the trade? How much do
they make? How do you become an expert on junk?
     In this project, we shall be investigating the local junk trade.
We shall be making slides and tape recordings, and shall be trying to produce a sound/vision record of what we discover.

P10   February 12th — February 23rd
      POISON, PILLS AND MORALS
      Tutors: Dr V. Wyatt and Albert Hunt

Recent discoveries in biology are changing our lives more than
most of us realise. The most obvious example is the contracep-
tive pill which has put biology into the middle of an argument
about morals.
     In this project we shall be looking at some recent discoveries
and asking how they affect life in Bradford. The courses will be
practical: no previous knowledge will be necessary.
     Dr Wyatt is Reader in Biology at the University of Bradford
and has recently been in Russia and the United States.

P11   February 19th — March 1st
      MAKING A CHANCE FILM
      Tutor: Peter Smailes

Since Freud discovered the unconscious, artists have increasingly recognised the element of chance in their work. This is particularly true of film-makers. Buñuel, for example, works by
association of images: he begins with one image, and this suggests to his mind another image. He builds up his films by following the lines of suggestion.
     Peter Smailes plans to make a film by following through
the associated ideas of a group. The group will begin with random images and try to develop them through free association.
It is hoped that the film will be ready to show at the end of
the Chance Festival (see P13).

P12   February 19th — March 1st
      MAKING A UNIVERSE
      Tutor: Colin Taylor

We shall begin by trying to make a model of our universe *as
we see it*. We shall then, by visiting Jodrell Bank and an obser-
vatory, find out about the universe as seen by experts, whose
ideas have been changed through recent discoveries, and go on
to make another model which corresponds more closely to
current ideas. We shall then go back and try to imagine the
universe as it was seen by people who imagined the earth was
at the centre of everything.
      The aim of the project will be to see how men's ideas about
the universe have changed; and how these changes have affected the way people live. Why, for instance, was the Church so
afraid of Galileo? Is there anything in recent discoveries that
is likely to affect established beliefs?
      This course will be mainly practical — but through the prac-
tical work we shall be exploring some of the most far-reaching
ideas in modern science.
      Colin Taylor is an Adult Education tutor in Shropshire, and
has worked in complementary studies at the Shrewsbury
School of Art.

P13   March 4th — March 15th
      FESTIVAL OF CHANCE
      Tutors: Peter Smailes, Bill Gainham, Albert Hunt
              and visiting celebrities.

This is a festival to celebrate the element of chance, which has
its own rules and its own logic.
      During the festival, we shall be looking at films by Buster
Keaton, Luis Buñuel and Jean Vigo
arranging a chance lecture
making
a chance band to perform a chance concert
a chance play
chance poems
chance paintings
chance designs
      If you would like to take part in any of these activities, we
invite you to join us in this chance project.

P14   March 18th — 29th
      THE WOMAN QUESTION
      Tutors: Ted and Betty Roszak

Women, we are told, are now free and equal. But how free are
they? And what use do they make of their freedom? To what

extent have men stopped regarding women as inferiors? What real changes have women's rights made in a man's world?

In this project, we shall look again at the place of women in our society, explore the obvious and subtle forms of subjugation, and study the effects of sexual stereotyping on our whole social structure.

The Roszaks teach at Berkeley University, San Francisco. They have had a good deal of experience of the civil rights movement in America; and they believe that there is a lot in common between American attitudes to women and to negroes. They will invite us to stop and look more closely at our own attitudes.

P15   March 25th — April 8th
WHAT DID WE LEARN?
Tutor: Bernard Bryan

Education in this country is supposed to develop the individual personality and to turn us into independent-minded people, critical of ourselves and of the society we belong to. But is this how education works? Are we really taught to think for ourselves? Or are we subtly conditioned, by all the pressures and routines of school life, to accept what we are told and fit in complacently wherever we find ourselves? Is our education system simply one of preparing the right pegs for the right holes?

In this project, we shall look carefully but critically at the way we have been educated, and try to discover the assumptions that have shaped our education. We shall examine school routines, as if they were the rituals of a strange society — the magic of the bell that rings every forty minutes, the mysterious ceremony of school assembly — and find out what these rituals tell us about attitudes in education.

Bernard Bryan is a lecturer at the Corby College of Education.

Summer Term

P16   April 22nd — May 3rd
THE STRIKE GAME
Tutors: John Golby, Bill Gainham, Albert Hunt

This is a follow-up to last year's very successful *Vietnam War Game.* We shall pretend that we are involved in an industrial enterprise which has labour troubles. A crisis will be invented, which will lead to an unofficial strike. There will be teams representing the strikers, the official Trades Unions, the management and the Government. We shall also need people to run a daily newsheet, and a broadcasting service.

Headquarters will be set up all over the college, and it will be part of the object of the players to convince non-playing students of the rightness of their case.

The main object will be simple — to win.

P17   April 22nd — May 3rd
MAKING A FILM
Tutor: Alan Lovell

Alan Lovell, of the British Film Institute, ran two popular film-making courses last year. The aim is not to produce a finished work of art, but to experiment with a movie camera and discover what can be done in film. If you wish to take part in this project — apply early.

P18   May 6th — May 17th
MAKING A RADIO BALLAD: THE GENERAL STRIKE IN
    BRADFORD
Tutors: John Golby and Stephen Brook

There are, in Bradford, a lot of people old enough to have taken part in the general strike. There are newspapers and photographs of the period. And then there are singers who remember the strike songs.

In this project, we shall try to build up a picture, in sound and vision, of the general strike as it affected Bradford. We shall make recordings of the people involved, relate local to national events, and analyse some of the changes that have occurred in the last forty years.

John Golby, who was the director of last year's project on *Bradford in 1910* is a tutor in the Extra-Mural Department of Southampton University, and an expert on social history.

P19   May 6th — May 17th
THE MAKING OF MOO
Tutors: Alan Dawe and Albert Hunt

In this project, we shall invent a religion.

Every religion must have a plausible system of belief, its own symbols, and its own ceremonies. We shall invent all these, make our own symbols and create our own rituals. We shall then try and convert other people, using any techniques of modern advertising that seem to be suitable.

Alan Dawe is a lecturer in sociology at the University of Leeds.

Albert Hunt (Senior Lecturer in Complementary Studies)

PLEASE FILL IN THIS FORM AND RETURN IT TO YOUR
HEAD OF SECTION IMMEDIATELY.

Name. . . . .

Department & Year. . . . .

I wish to enrol for one of the following projects.

1)

2)

3)

(State your first THREE choices in order of preference)

Appendix Three

A complete account of the putting-together of a Theatre Group show
has already been given in the introduction to *John Ford's Cuban
Missile Crisis* (published by Eyre Methuen). This appendix consists
of a scene from *Looking Forward to 1942*, together with some ex-
planation of how the scene was created.

Looking Forward to 1942 was the culmination of three years'
work. It took the form of a pentecostal meeting, and tried to create
all the genuine excitement of such a meeting. It began with swinging choruses and free shouting, and moved through prayers, testimonies, healings and a sermon to an emotionally overwhelming
appeal to sinners.

Into the testimonies, the war material was woven. Much of this
was local — consisting of the testimonies of the people of Bradford
and Liverpool. But these were set against the wider issues, which
were explored in the testimonies of Neville Chamberlain, Adolf
Eichmann and Sir Arthur Harris. Throughout the second half of the
show, events were dominated by the figure of Churchill, who controlled the actors with a whistle, and sat throughout, drinking brandy,
smoking a cigar, and painting a landscape, which was auctioned off
at the end of each performance. He painted this picture, while
Eichmann destroyed eight million Jews, and Harris burned Dresden.

It was in the handling of these major figures that the 1942 show made its political points. In a mock boxing match, the usual judgement on Chamberlain was questioned; and in the second act the testimonies of Eichmann and Harris were set side by side. And the role of Churchill himself was re-examined in what D. A. N. Jones, in *The Listener*, described as 'a dramatic alternative to Hochhuth'.

The scene printed here comes at the end of the first act, and deals with the coming to power of Churchill in 1940. It provides an example of the way all the elements used in the creation of the show were brought together in performance.

LOOKING FORWARD TO 1942?

THE ORDINATION SCENE

Throughout the show, the set remains basically the same. At the back of the stage and in the centre there is a huge puppet-box. It stands high above the stage and is built in such a way that when a live actor pops up inside, only his head is visible. This box — which could also be seen as a pulpit — is used at various times during the show: in the reading of the word of God; the testimonies of Eichmann and Harris; and the sermon.

In front of the box are two lines of chairs, stretching to the front of the stage. The chairs are facing each other, so that the actors — the Saints — are seen by the audience in a half-sideways view. Most of the action takes place between these lines of chairs.

The Saints are wearing 1940s dress — but each Saint has his own variation. Thus, one actor (MAC) has a gangster hat and carries a wooden gun. DOUG, who plays Chamberlain, has a dinner suit without a shirt. KEITH wears a blue serge, which is torn at the knee and has a flower in his button-hole. (All the actors are here named by their own names, i.e. the names of the students who created the roles.)

From the beginning, the Saints carry home-made musical instruments, e.g. one has a bicycle chain, another a tin can with pebbles inside, another the wooden pipe off an old organ. CHRIS has a pill bottle with a ball-bearing inside. DOUG has a tambourine. Just off-stage, but visible, there is a girl (SALLY) who punctuates the action with bangs on two tambourines and a gong. At the beginning of the Ordination scene, most of the Saints are kneeling about the stage. They have been giving the testimonies of the evacuees. MAURICE and KEITH are hidden behind the puppet-box.

CHRIS. *Speaks in gibberish.* JOHN *(As Pastor) comes forward.*

JOHN. I think God has sent us a message in the form of tongues. Can anyone give an interpretation?

DOUG. *(As Chamberlain) rises to his feet: but before he can begin to speak,* KEITH *has popped up in the puppet box to take the words out of his mouth.*

KEITH. The Prime Minister has appealed for sacrifice. The nation is prepared for any sacrifice so long as it has leadership. I say solemnly that the Prime Minister should show an example of sacrifice. Because there is nothing which could contribute more to victory in this war than that he should sacrifice his seals of office.

JOHN (To DOUG). You have stood here too long for all the good you have been doing. In the name of God, go. (DOUG *wanders sulkily back to his seat.*) And now, Brother Maurice, perhaps you would bring some order and sanity back into this meeting.

MAURICE *emerges, slowly and impressively, from behind the puppet box. He is big, well-built, with a somewhat large belly. He wears a blue striped suit, but no shirt. He also wears football socks outside his trousers, and ballet shoes. He has a mass of long, wild, unruly hair. He advances to the centre of the stage and speaks very quietly.*

MAURICE. Shall we all return to our seats and bow our heads in silent prayer?

THE SAINTS *go back to their seats and bow their heads. After some seconds,* CHRIS *stands up and speaks direct to the audience.*

CHRIS. During the early years of the pentecostal movement there were no leaders. Small groups of Saints gathered together in upper rooms, over bakeries, above shops and garages, to worship the Lord, to be filled with the Spirit, to speak with other tongues. But God showed the need to evangelise and he rose up great men to take the pentecostal message all round the world.

At this point a drum begins to beat slowly and during the rest of CHRIS's *speech* THE SAINTS *ceremoniously dress* MAURICE, *begining with a long impresario's coat in camel, lined with fur — and a tin helmet.*

CHRIS. The greatest of these was Principal George Jeffreys, the founder of the Elim Foursquare Gospel Alliance who, throughout the 1920s, carried out mass evangelism in the towns and cities of Britain.

An easel and paints are set out in front of the puppet box.

CHRIS. His campaigns reached a climax on Good Friday, 1928, when, at the Royal Albert Hall, in front of 10,000 pentecostals, Principal Jeffreys immersed in water 1,000 believers.

MAURICE *is given a brandy glass.*

CHRIS. Two spotlights shone on Principal Jeffreys as he stood waist deep in a specially constructed galvanised iron tank. (MAURICE *is given a bottle of brandy.*) The tank was surrounded by imitation grass, roses, lilies, palms and other plants. An inflow and outflow enabled the water to represent the flowing of the River Jordan. (MAURICE *is given a huge cigar.*) The procession of candidates came on to the stage, passed through the tank and wound up wet and ecstatic. (*Drum stops.* CHRIS *sits down.*)

MAURICE *is now left in the centre of the stage and we see that he has been turned into Churchill — the actions have gone on all the time* CHRIS *was speaking. He lights his cigar, pours a glass of brandy, goes and sits in front of the easel and picks up a paint brush. Then again he speaks quietly.*

MAURICE. Brother John. Brother Keith.

JOHN *and* KEITH *go and stand to attention either side of* MAURICE.

MAURICE. Shall we have the testimonies of the people of Liverpool now?

THE SAINTS *all pick up their instruments and begin to play them loudly and without any fixed rhythm. The sound goes on, rather like the roaring of a factory machine. After a time* MAC *comes to the front of the stage and stops playing his instrument. The others go on and he speaks above the noise.*

MAC. The Germans could always find their way to Liverpool because of the railway lights left on during the blackout.

He puts his instrument on the stage and sits behind it. As each SAINT *comes to give a testimony, the same procedure is followed, so that the sound of the music grows less and less with each testimony.*

NEIL. A group of children lost in the sewers were mistaken for German invaders.

DOUG. Fire-engines travelling along bomb-damaged streets sometimes fell into craters.

JACQUI. To save Pickford's vans from being destroyed, the families of Bootle drove them out into the countryside every night and slept in them. The next morning they came back into the city to work. It was an offence to miss a morning's work.

By this time only two instruments are playing: STEPHANIE *is rhythmically shaking a chain:* CHRIS *is rattling his bottle.* STEPHANIE *comes to the front of the stage and stops playing. Only* CHRIS's *bottle is now heard.*

STEPHANIE. Soldiers, going abroad, had to march down the bomb-damaged streets. They were very moved by the spirit of the Liverpool people.

CHRIS *goes on playing bottle, comes front stage, stops playing, and speaks in the silence.*

CHRIS. In May 1941, some people on Bootle were seen walking down the street carrying white flags.

He sits down. All except JOHN, KEITH, *and* MAURICE *are now sitting in a line at the front of the stage.* KEITH *and* JOHN *are still standing to attention either side of* MAURICE. MAURICE *goes on painting in the silence. Sips brandy.*

MAURICE. Now. Things have been a bit sloppy until now. What we need is some new church rules. Brother Keith! (*Hands paper to* KEITH.) Read out the new church rules.

KEITH *marches to front of stage: Reads in a military voice.*

KEITH. The Government has the authority to repeal any act of Parliament: can censor all letters: can imprison without trial. It is an offence to disguise your nationality, change your name without permission, hoard food, blow whistles, fly kites, fly balloons, ring bells, sound sirens.

KEITH *puts paper away.* MAURICE *paints. Pause.*

MAURICE. Brother Keith, I now name you Ernest Bevin, and put you in charge of war work.

MAURICE *goes on painting.* KEITH *shouts.*

KEITH. All right. You've all had it easy until now, but I'm going to tighten things up. You two: down the mines. You two: dig for victory. You two: munitions. Attention! Sit down again. Faster! Attention! Right turn! Quick March! Over here! And now, start working. And sing as you work.

THE SAINTS *have marched to the chairs stage right and formed into twos. They now sing and mime work in time to the song.*

SAINTS.   Marching in chorus, Jesus before us
            Foursquare Gospel workers are we:
            Though men may taunt us, nothing can daunt us,
            On then to victory.
            Jesus the Saviour . . .

MAURICE *blows whistle. All freeze.*

MAURICE. Brother John. I now name you Lord Beaverbrook and put you in charge of aircraft production.

JOHN *selects three of the* SAINTS *and directs them to the other line of chairs, stage left.*

JOHN. You, you, and you, over there. Now the war effort depends on you, so I want you to work hard and sing along.

DOUG, STEPHANIE and NEIL *start aircraft mime. The others, stage right, remain frozen.* KEITH *wanders across stage, noticing that three of his workers have disappeared.*

DOUG.   Give me oil in my lamp, oil in my lamp,
STEPHANIE. Oil in my lamp, I pray
NEIL.   Give me oil in my lamp,
               Keep me shining in the camp,
               Until the break of day.
               Give me oil in my lamp . . .

MAURICE *whistles.* SAINTS *freeze.*

KEITH. He's taken half my workers.

MAURICE. Oh, well, they'll just have to work twice as hard, won't they.

Whistle. The two groups now sing rival choruses and work. JOHN *compares his workers with* KEITH'S. *Whistle.*

JOHN. Now, I've been watching the other workers in war industry and they're working twice as hard as you are. So I want you to work five times as hard as they do.

MAURICE *whistles. The two groups start singing and working. They sing louder and louder, rival songs, and work more and more frantically, encouraged by* JOHN *and* KEITH *who shout, 'More munitions! More bombers!' The action of the stage becomes totally frenetic. When it reaches a climax,* MAURICE *blows his whistle. All freeze.* MAURICE *comes slowly between the frozen groups towards the front of the stage. He speaks, but not in a Churchillian voice. Very cool and unemotional.*

MAURICE. So at last the trade unionists cast their slowly-framed, jealously guarded rules and privileges on the altar where wealth, rank, privilege and property had already been laid. (*Sips brandy*) I was much in harmony with Bevin and Beaverbrook during the white-hot weeks. Later they quarrelled, which was a pity. But at this climax we were all together. I cannot speak too highly of the loyalty of Mr Chamberlain, or of the resolution of my cabinet colleagues. Let me give them my salute. (*Puffs cigar*) And now, get this rabble out of here. Not you, Brother Chris, Brother John!

JOHN. Brother Keith!

KEITH. Squad, attention! Right and left turn! Quick March!

THE SAINTS *march off back stage.* JOHN *and* KEITH *follow them.* CHRIS *remains where he is.*

MAURICE. Ah, Brother Chris. (CHRIS *comes forward and stands behind the musical instruments which have been left in a line at the front of the stage.*) Ah, Brother Chris. I don't want you to think that your work for the war effort has gone un-noticed. As a reward for your work, I now promote you to . . . (MAURICE *contemplates musical instruments, picks up bicycle chain, dangles it from* CHRIS's *shoulder.*) Montgomery? No. (*Replaces bicycle chain, puts tin can on* CHRIS's *head.*) The King? No. (*Replaces tin can, walks along line of instruments: Picks up* CHRIS's *pill bottle.* CHRIS *yawns.* MAURICE *pushes pill bottle into* CHRIS's *mouth.*) Lord Cherwell. And from now on you're my chief scientific adviser for the rest of the war.

MAURICE *walks back and starts painting again.* CHRIS *follows him slowly. Until the end of the scene,* CHRIS *speaks with a bottle in his mouth.* CHRIS *watches* MAURICE *paint.*

CHRIS. Hold your brush like this: as if it were a gun. (MAURICE *paints.*) I've been thinking, Winnie, about all those troops on the beaches at Dunkirk. I think they need some entertainment. We could send the Windmill Girls over. You know, all naked. They could dance on the beaches like this. (*Demonstrates dancing girls.*) What else could we do? We could send Vera Lynn. She could sing that song of hers (*Sings, waving his arms crooner fashion.*) 'We'll meet again, don't know where, don't know when. . .' Or we could send that comedian: you know, the one that always begins his turn by saying 'As I was on my way to Dunkirk. . .' Ha, Ha. Wha' else could we do?

MAURICE. Do you like my painting?

CHRIS. A bit more yellow over there. I've been negotiating with the BBC to play music. For two reasons. (*Holds up two fingers in vulgar V-sign.*) First for unhealthy people who just can't keep fit while they're working for the war. We can put music on early in the morning and they could do exercises. Like this. (*Does gymnastics and sings.*) 'We're gonna hang out the washing on the Siegfried Line. . .' And secondly, for all those bored housewives who just don't know what to do while the bombs are dropping — they could line up all the tea-cups like this, and stir. (*Sings and stirs.*) 'Run, rabbit, run, rabbit, run, run, run.' Oh, and I've been thinking. Now that you're Prime Minister and all that, don't you think you ought to make a few speeches. (MAURICE *looks up with interest.*) Do you like that? I've been thinking up a few ideas. You could begin (*Very offhand.*) 'Never in the field of human endeavour has so little been done by so many for, er, so many.' Something like that. Juggle it round a bit. And you could end with something romantic. 'We will fight them on the beaches. . . ' That should get 'em going. Do you like that? I'll tell you what. Why don't you try it. 'Never in the field of human endeavour. . . '

MAURICE (*Quietly.*) 'Never in the field of human endeavour. . .'

CHRIS. No, No, not like that. Get some feeling into it. (*Puts on Churchillian growl, distorted by bottle.*) '*Nevah,* in the *field* of human *endeavah.* . .' (*Opens* MAURICE's *coat, pats him on belly.*) Let it come from your diaphragm.

MAURICE. (*Imitating Churchill.*) 'Nevah, in the field of human endeavah. . .'

CHRIS. 'Nevah' to rhyme with 'Endeavah'.

MAURICE. 'Nevah'; 'Endevah'.

CHRIS. That's right. 'Has so little. . .'

MAURICE. 'Has so little . . .'

CHRIS. '. . . been done by so many . . .'

MAURICE. '. . . been done by so many . . .'

CHRIS. '. . . for so many . . .'

MAURICE. '. . . for so many . . .'

CHRIS. I'll tell you what. (*Produces mirror from behind puppet box.*) Practise it in front of this mirror. (*Places mirror down on the stage leaning against one of the chairs.*)

MAURICE. (*Crouching to see himself.*) 'Never in the field of human endeavour. . .'

CHRIS. Get your cigar in.

CHRIS *forces* MAURICE *to his knees, rides on* MAURICE's *back.* MAURICE *struggles with brandy glass and cigar. Echoes speech after* CHRIS, *now sounding* very *Churchillian.*)

MAURICE (*on knees*). 'Never in the field of human endeavour has so little been done by so many for so many. Never in the field of human endeavour. . .

CHRIS (*Jumping off* MAURICE *and leaving stage.*) Try to say it as if you meant it. (*Goes.*)

MAURICE. 'Never in the field of human endeavour . . .' or 'conflict': 'Conflict . . . has so little been done by so many for so many. Or few. Never in the field . . .'

He picks up mirror and carries it back to painting. Balances mirror on his knee. Tries to paint, drink brandy, smoke cigar and practise speech in mirror all at the same time. Lights slowly dim.

COMMENTARY

The opening section of the scene — the 'speaking in tongues' — is taken from observation of such phenomena during the *Hot Gospel* project.

The speeches by Keith and John ('The Prime Minister has appealed for sacrifice. . . . You have stood here too long. . . .') are taken from the Parliamentary debate in which Chamberlain was overthrown.

Maurice Burgess invented the bizarre costume in which he appeared from behind the puppet box, and over which the regalia of Churchill was to be draped.

The speech about the pentecostal movement, by Chris, is an adaptation from a 1930s biography of George Jeffreys, the leader of Elim Foursquare Alliance: the episodes described (e.g. the rally at the Albert Hall) are all factually correct.

The 'testimonies of the people of Liverpool' were all recorded by students during a week's visit to Liverpool, in which they recorded, in particular, stories by people who had been bombed in Bootle (and, incidentally, talked to the people in Bootle pubs about the bombing of Dresden).

Keith's speech about 'discipline' ('The Government has the authority to repeal' etc.) is a direct quote from a government proclamation of 1940, unearthed during a complementary studies project called *Living in Wartime*.

The song, 'Marching in Chorus', together with, 'Give me oil in my lamp', is taken from *Elim Choruses*, which we bought during the *Hot Gospel* project.

The battle between 'Bevin' and 'Beaverbrook' ('He's taken half my workers') was taken from accounts unearthed during the *Living in Wartime* project.

The Churchill speech ('So at last the trade unionists. . . .') is a quote from Churchill's memoirs: the stage direction, in which Churchill drinks brandy, while calling for sacrifices, seemed to us an accurate image of the way of life depicted in those memoirs.

The comedy scene between 'Lindemann' and 'Churchill' at the end of the act drew on popular culture (*Music while you work*), on what was known of the relationship between Lindemann and Churchill, and on what was also known of Churchill's rehearsal techniques, in front of a mirror. The conscious aim was to alienate a familiar speech by putting it into a music-hall context. Audiences everywhere recognised the speech — and found the context very funny.

The whole scene demonstrates the way in which elements from local projects (*Hot Gospel* and *Living in Wartime*) could be fused together with historical material to create a statement that would equally entertain audiences in Bradford, in Liverpool, in small towns like Selby, in Amsterdam (where the audience started talking about Brecht), in Zagreb (where the show won all the major awards at an international festival), and in Wroclaw, Poland, where the audience was very conscious of what had happened in 1939 — and was delighted that a British group should be willing to examine Britain's role critically and satirically.

What must be stressed about the 1942 show is that all this different material didn't come together in a few day's work. A great deal of personal research went into the project — which was reflected in the density of the final production.

Appendix Four

It's stupid when you have to go to school
And try to show them something and they think you're just a fool
Because all they want to see is what they've seen before.
And all you have to do
Is just a little more
Than what you ever do
Yes it's a drag.
And it's stupid when you have to go to town
And you want to do better
Than walking up and down
Looking at the things that they want you to see.
Because all there is to see
Is what you've seen before
And all they ever ask
Is just a little more
Than what you want to pay
Yes it's a drag.
And it's stupid when you go out at nights
And all that ever happens
Is they turn out the lights.
And all they ever do
Is what you've done before
And all they ever want
Is just a little more
Than you're prepared to give
Yes it's a drag.
And it's stupid when you have to die
And every one goes to church
And every one has to cry
And all they ever want
Is just a little more
Of that gay vivacious person
That you were before
You became such a drag.
And even at your funeral
There's not enough gin
So we'll all go to a pub
And get some bottles in
And we'll all try to drink
Just a little more
Than we've ever managed
To drink before
But it's a drag.

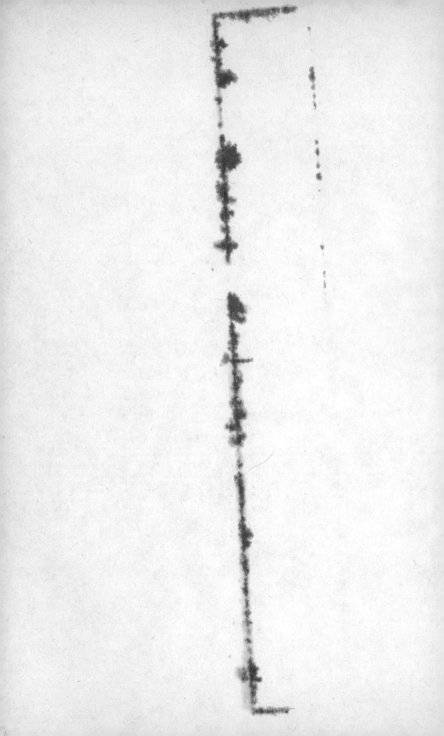